Young in the Spirit

Young in the Spirit

Spiritual Strengthening for Seniors and Caregivers

To arlene,
Wishing you many
blessings.
Love,
Mary

Mary K. Doyle

3E
3E PRESS

Geneva, IL

Young in the Spirit
Spiritual Strengthening for Seniors and Caregivers
by Mary K. Doyle

Edited by L. C. Fiore
Cover design by Chuck Romano

Published by 3E Press
Distributed by ACTA Publications, 4848 N. Clark St., Chicago, IL
60640. 1-800-897-2282

Library of Congress Control Number: 2013932227

ISBN: 978-0-9677449-5-7

Printed in the United States of America by United Graphics Incorporation

Contents

Appendix

Dedication

This book is dedicated to my parents, John and Patricia Doyle, who showed their children how to live and die to the Lord. (Romans 14:8)

My soul is like a weaned child with its mother (Psalm 131);
young in the spirit of the Lord.

Face of an Aging World

"Psalm 118, do you know it?"

My husband and I were on a return flight from his brother's memorial service. I sat in the middle seat. The young man next to me said that he was going to The University of North Carolina at Greensboro for an interview in hopes of enrolling in a graduate degree program. His smile and exuberance drew me out of my somber mood. We chatted about courses of study. I told him I had a Master's degree in Theology.

After take-off the young traveler moved to an open row but later returned to tap me on the shoulder. He showed me a blurb in a magazine. It said that Tim Howard, the American soccer goalie for Everton of England and the United States national team, had a favorite Bible verse from Psalm 118.

"Do you know it?" the young man pressed.

I laughed and explained to him that there are 150 psalms, and I hadn't memorized them all. I pulled out my little travel Bible that contains the New Testament, Psalms, and Proverbs, opened to Psalm 118 and handed it to him. Howard is particularly fond of verse 24 which reads, "This is the day that the LORD has/made;/let us rejoice and be glad in it." We talked about the psalm briefly, but the plane's engine noises and the people squeezing past as they moved up and down the aisle made it difficult to hear. But, the experience stirred my curiosity. I wanted to study the psalm more closely.

As many Christians know, it isn't unusual to be thumbing through the Bible only to find that the first passage to strike our attention is the one message we need at that time. This also occasionally happens when a verse is posted on a sign or quoted somewhere. In whatever way one catches our eye, the Holy Spirit is talking to us and asking us to take note of it.

Rarely does a total stranger ask someone about a particular Scripture verse. I believe I connected with the young man on that flight to draw both of our attentions to the message in Psalm 118. To an extent, it connects us to Howard, also, because he was unabashed to publicly acknowledge his faith and devotion to the Lord. And if he hadn't stated the significance of the psalm's message to him, it's not likely that I would be bringing it to your attention right now. God is speaking to all of us, and when that happens in such a pointed way, it is a good idea to listen.

The fundamental message of Psalm 118 is to appreciate and enjoy the present. The timing was especially poignant for me as I was returning from a funeral, and because I am a caregiver to a loved one with Alzheimer's disease, an illness that holds its victim in the now. As Alzheimer's progresses, the past slips away and the future is a concept that is difficult, if not impossible, to comprehend. Focus remains solely in the moment. As one moment passes it vanishes forever and is replaced by the next.

The disease also results in a mounting state of mourning for those who are close by. The slow death of their loved one's memories and abilities is painful to watch. In addition, the loved one's endless repetition of questions and statements, their odd and often dangerous behavior, and their confusion over basic concepts try the caregiver's patience.

I am fully aware that my loved one's illness has at least as much to do with me as it does him. I believe that God is offering many lessons for me to learn. Typically, I am an organizer and a planner. I like things sorted into categories and set up in advance. But no longer are my days typical, organized, or planned. Few things work out as anticipated, and my "to do" list is abandoned and replaced with living in the moment with my loved one. As I walk the journey of Alzheimer's, I am learning to appreciate what God is revealing and so generously presenting at the time. Little on my list of scheduled activities is nearly as important or even necessary as I previously thought. I'm learning to heed the message of Psalm 118 and be happy in the glorious day that God has made.

Life is a God-given gift. Every moment of every day is precious and holy because without God's blessing, we would not exist. From birth to death, our time on Earth is to be treasured and appreciated. This can be difficult to remember as we age and encounter the changes that naturally occur—both physical and mental. It isn't always easy to be happy when we are in pain or saddened by the loss of a loved one.

Our society suffers from a dichotomy; we fear aging while we search for longevity. Rather than reveal our true age as evidence of God's generosity, we try to mask or alter any sign of it. Our culture maintains that a youthful appearance and vitality is essential at all stages of life.

No one should suspect that we are as old as we are. We want to live a very long life, and we are in fact doing so, but we don't want to experience any signs of the passage of time. It as if aging itself is a disease or failure on our part.

Across society efforts to appear more youthful are accelerating as the population ages in unprecedented numbers. We are getting older by the minute, not only individually but globally as well. More people are living far into their senior years and will continue to do so, gradually increasing the percentage of older people in the world.

In addition, women worldwide are having fewer babies resulting in a declining population under 15 years of age. Fertility rates are at 2.75 children per woman and are expected to continue to fall closer to 2. With the combination of low birth rates and increased longevity, studies project that by the year 2050 all developed countries are expected to have a median age of more than 40 years. The average age for Japan, the country with the oldest population in the world, will be 55. So as we age, we'll have a lot of company.

At the onset of the twentieth century the average lifespan was 47 years (Rowe, 4). Although many lived far beyond that, many more died young due to accidents and illnesses that went undiagnosed or were untreatable at the time. Today, more than a century later, we are outliving our ancestors by decades. According to data gathered by the government's National Center for Health Statistics, the average baby born in 2006 was projected to live 78 years. And this average continues to increase. By the year 2050, the average life expectancy is believed to reach the age of 85. That is nearly double the lifetime of people living only a few generations earlier.

The phenomenon is not isolated to our country. *Zenit*, the Catholic online newsletter, recently stated that this is so for countries all over the world. In fact, 30 other countries have a greater life expectancy than the United States. Japan has the longest life expectancy at 83 years for children born in 2006 (World Health Organization data).

This blessing of an extended life prompts several questions. Researchers want to know why this is happening. How can we promote not only our longevity but more importantly, better living? What's more, there is a spiritual component in all of this. Not only does spirituality promote longevity, it affects our quality of life, and of course, the path on which we travel into our afterlife. For this reason it also is important that we investigate how to strengthen our faith to carry us through the challenges of aging and prepare for the journey to our eternal rest.

Stereotypes and Prejudices

We are deficient in handling the emotions we attach to aging. We don't even have adequate words to define the later years.

Other age groups are clearly classified with names such as infancy, babyhood, childhood, adolescence, teens, young adulthood, and middle-age. These terms note a specific period lasting anywhere from several months to a couple of decades at most. The classification for the years after middle age is less descriptive. Retirement age, or rather the age when one is considered to be a senior, varies greatly among companies and organizations. Some define seniors as early as age 50. The US Government is changing its noted retirement age; today it is 65 years old for those born prior to 1943; 66 for those born from 1943 to 1955; and the number increases slightly after that.

Regardless, we typically define people who are 65 years of age or more as *old*. Although there is no doubt that the person is not young, the *old* label is grossly insufficient—and vague. It does not recognize the extensive diversity that exists in a period that encompasses four or more decades. *Old* also conjures impressions of being beyond our prime or usefulness. When a car, clothing, or piece of furniture is old, we refer to it with flattering terms such as antique, vintage, and classic. We need that type of expression for people of advanced age.

The term *elderly* is often used, but this is really an adjective, not a noun. *Elder* is more grammatically correct but infers wisdom and intelligence, which may not be so. *Seniors* or *senior citizens* are better, although they may be confused with a senior in high school or college or an employee of many years. And again, these words are used to cover an extensive time period. (I will refer to people aged 65 or more in several ways including *older* or *older people, elders,* and *seniors.* Please know that whatever term I use, I use with the utmost respect.)

Women are sometimes more sensitive to language. Whereas many men normally define themselves by what they do, many women tend to assume the world defines them by how they look. Our face reveals the story of our life, so it must look young for us to be perceived as desirable. Perhaps this is because society seems to appreciate older men more so than women. Many senior men are recognized as distinguished, experienced, knowledgeable, and powerful. They continue to attract women of all ages. Fewer similar opportunities are awarded senior women.

But widespread stereotypes about the aging of both men and women exist. Every industry sees it. Evidence is found even in the medical field, according to Dr. Jonathan Leiff, Chief of Geriatrics at Lemuel Ahattuck Hospital. Dr. Leiff stated in an article entitled, "Eight Reasons Why Doctors Fear the Elderly, Chronic Illness and Death" (Lieff, 1982) that first-year medical students show prejudice toward senior patients. It is not unusual for them to refer to these patients with negative terms. Dr. Leiff believes the behavior stems from the doctors' own unresolved feelings about aging.

This may well be so. Our society has little exposure to aging, dying, and death, and therefore, also little understanding of it. Until the last few decades, several generations lived together in one home. Children and grandchildren observed the aging of elderly family members on a daily basis. Now this scenario is rare. Not only do older generations not live in the same household as their children, they live far away. The trend for seniors to reside in communities restricted to their age group secludes them from the rest of the world even more, although there is some swing back to multi-generational households due to the low employment rate and the economic instability of recent years.

Exposure to older people is vitally important to all of us but especially to the younger generations. Through such opportunities we gain a better expectation of what we may encounter and do to age "successfully." We can witness firsthand the natural progression of human life. We also observe role models who use God's gift of life to the fullest extent of their time on this earth.

Typically, older people are understood to be no longer attractive and feeble in mind and body. Seniors need care and cannot provide it themselves. This line of thinking disregards the fact that, as with all ages, there are many ways to be old. There is a wide range of capabilities among people in the 65 and older category.

One's age is not indicative of their ability. An 80 year-old may continue working productively while someone in her 70s needs assistance bathing and walking short distances. Variances also occur throughout one's senior years. An individual may have several years that require significant support and others that are rich in strength and ability. And those periods of need versus independence may not come in any particular order.

In fact, a good number of today's seniors are quite active. Many are working part or full time or participating in regularly scheduled athletic activities such as golf, dance, and swimming. They take good care of themselves and are fully aware of the need to maintain a nutritious diet and seek medical attention when necessary. They also are exposed to health education classes at local hospitals, community college, and public libraries.

Several years ago I spoke on the topic of mentoring to a women's leadership program at Dominican University in River Forest, Illinois. Students were asked to bring their mentors to the last session and introduce them to the class. Two of the mentors were more than 90 years of age. Both were stunning women dressed impeccably. They told impressive accounts of their *current* employment and activities. One woman held a political position. The other, legally blind, was a successful entrepreneur.

Those mentors inspired all of us and offered a possibility for our own future, one much richer than most of us previously imagined. They proved we can reach out and share our knowledge, wisdom, contacts, and talent every day of our life until the last. We, like them, have so much to offer. Allowing access to what we learned and gained from our time here is a gift we give of ourselves to the next generations.

Impact of Global Aging

Living a long life is definitely less desirable if you are
financially, physically, or emotionally depleted. A larger,
older global population will result in a world with different
needs, concerns, and benefits. Its impact will be realized
financially, medically, socially, and spiritually. Modifications
will be required to adequately accommodate the needs of the
new society.

Aging obviously makes a significant impact on us physically.
Health is most meaningful to older people because we
understand its direct correlation with quality of life. Few of us
reach our senior years without some ailment. Hypertension,
diabetes, high cholesterol, osteoporosis, vision and hearing
impairment, joint deterioration, diminished memory, and
chronic pain or discomfort may surface with the breakdown of
the human body. Much of our later years are typically devoted
to attending to these illnesses and disabilities.

Caregiving is another point to consider. Women are the
majority of people over 65 years of age, so it is no surprise that
we also comprise the majority of caregivers as well as those
needing care. Women will most likely care for parents, siblings,
or a spouse before and into our own senior years. We must
also consider who will care for us, should the need arise.

Another issue women face is that we tend to have more
serious financial concerns with age than most men. Evidence
shows that older women are at greater financial risk as our
gender comprises three-fourths of the elderly poor. Fifty-nine
percent of nonwhite women over 85 live below the poverty
line (GOC 122). The causes of such a tremendous economic
disadvantage are many. But in short, women live longer than
men and do so with significantly lower retirement savings. It's
quite a challenge to save enough money to support oneself for
the 30 or 40 years after retirement.

Few women will receive a pension great enough to carry
them through their remaining years. As of this writing, women

typically earn less than 80 cents to a man's dollar for the same work, so our earning potential while working and the corresponding pension is 20 percent less than a man's. The death of a spouse, chronic illness, Social Security biased toward singles over couples, discrimination in the workplace during earlier periods of employment, and years of unpaid service to the family as homemaker, stay-at-home mother, and elder caregiver minimizes the opportunity to build an adequate retirement reserve.

Statistics gathered by the organization OWL claim that women are less than half as likely to receive any pension or health insurance. Those who do, typically receive only half as much as men. Life-long status as a single person, divorce, and death of a spouse also challenge the economic status of women. Two-thirds of all women over 65 live alone, in contrast to one-fourth of the male population.

Once a spouse dies, the remaining spouse's income is instantly, and often significantly, reduced. In addition, if the deceased person was married more than once, his estate will likely be divided among his children from the previous marriage as well as their joint children and the surviving spouse. This typically occurs at a point in a woman's life when she no longer can work or may have few marketable skills. She is left with limited resources and ability to increase her income.

Longevity drains society's collective financial resources as well. The country's Social Security system is in crisis. An increase in life expectancy combined with decreasing birth rates results in fewer workers contributing to Social Security which financially supports seniors. By 2050 Europe will have the lowest support at 1.4 working persons for every dependent. North America will be right behind with only 1.6 contributing workers. This is a serious situation, as one-third of all Americans aged 65 years or more say that Social Security benefits comprise nearly all of their income.

One recommendation that is periodically raised suggests a cap on Medicare and Medicaid so younger citizens won't be denied the care they'll eventually need. (Medicare and Medicaid pay a significant portion of seniors' medical expenses, and there is some question as to how much will be left in the "pot" once the younger generation retires.) This theory claims that the young are our future and so have so much more to live for. Because our society measures personal value by productivity, if someone is too old to produce in a marketable fashion they do not deserve public funding.

This concept deems aging an economic burden. Such an attitude is particularly threatening for those whose financial security is already threatened. But it doesn't account for the fact that the *old* person in question may live years, or even decades, past retirement. And many are very productive in their senior years.

In addition, this idea sets a dangerous spiritual precedent of judging the worthiness of those individuals receiving care. It disregards that all life is God-given and precious. There should be no expiration date for medical attention—or social attention, for that matter. Everyone deserves public respect and care as long as the Holy Spirit, the Lord, the giver of life, breathes life into us.

Young in the Spirit of the Lord

Getting to a ripe old age is only half of the longevity equation. We not only want to live longer but healthier and happier as well. It is little consolation to make it to the age of 90 or more if we are suffering and miserable. The goal is to achieve that age while being physically, mentally, emotionally, and spiritually strong. And the spiritual component is important in making everything work.

We have much to contemplate in this regard. Our advanced years are sure to be (or are) a mix of pain and relief, difficulties and pleasure, sorrow and joy. If we aren't a senior yet, it is a good idea to do our best to physically and financially prepare for the future. Once we are in this stage, or cannot do anymore to prepare, there is little purpose in fretting over our condition.

Aches and pains and other outward signs indicate the body is aging and serve as daily reminders to move away from thoughts of this life. The body is a temporary vessel and a temple for the Holy Spirit. Our soul exists eternally and therefore demands greater attention. Building our faith and our relationship with God is the priority, more so in our later years than any other time of our life.

We cannot know exactly where we are on our life journey. We may be 42 years old reading this book in anticipation of our second half of life; 68 years old on the cusp of old age with only one more year remaining; or 95 with another ten. In any case, with each passing moment, we certainly are one step closer to the threshold of our eternal rest. Without a doubt, the older we are, the nearer we are to our death. If we haven't begun to invest in our spiritual health, there is no time like the present. The moment that we will we cross over is fast approaching.

Nurturing faith then becomes increasingly more important with age. Our relationship with the Lord must grow and deepen until our last breath. This book offers points to contemplate and some suggestions as to how this can be done. The information comes from Scripture, respected theological, psychological, and social works, and personal thoughts from adults of middle to senior ages. Take these ideas as they are or modify them to what works best for you.

You also are encouraged on your quest for a better relationship with the Lord, to call on the Holy Spirit for guidance and inspiration. Ask that your faith be fully awakened. Set your mind on the Spirit so that you will have life and peace (Romans 8:6). The Holy Spirit is sure to inspire and lead you, a child of God (Romans 8:14), forever young in the Spirit.

And don't forget to treasure every moment along the way. If you're like I am and need to be reminded of this, don't worry. You will be told again. Everywhere I look I see the

verse from Psalm 118. Although I care for someone with
Alzheimer's, I must be the one in need of repetition. Heavenly
messengers continue to proclaim God's abundant goodness
and generosity by whispering in my ear, "This is the day that
the LORD has/made;/let us rejoice and be glad in it."

Veni Sancte Spiritus. Come Holy Spirit.
Fire the desire within me to continuously move closer to you.

Spirituality for Better Living

Face lifts, knee replacements, liposuction, and a cornucopia of medications. Our aging society is obsessed with looking, feeling, and staying young. The quest is on for the magical Fountain of Youth, and we do indeed seem to be accomplishing this. The segment of the population who are 65 years of age and older is rapidly increasing. And it will continue to do so.

This increased interest in aging has prompted numerous studies on just how longevity is attained. Scientists want to understand the fundamentals of a fit and joyful long life and are finding a number of contributing factors. According to the Gerontology Project, an Atlanta-based research group, more than 100,000 people worldwide are more than 100 years old. From this group they also estimate about 450 people are at least 110 years of age. These people are particularly important to researchers. From them researchers are learning how we too can follow the path of longevity.

Keys to Longevity

Repeatedly, research shows that the same important factors arise. Longevity is the result of several streams pooling together. Genetics, a strong social network, balanced nutrition, exercise, a solid foundation of spirituality, limited stress, optimism, and a sense of humor contribute. Advances in science, health-care, and sanitation also play a significant role. Nearly everyone in the United States has access to quality drinking water and sewage systems. This is a tremendous boon to our overall health.

Genetics is perhaps the deepest well from which that fountain of youth draws. The director of the University of the Miami Center on Aging, Dr. Carl Eisdorfer, MD, says that our genetic makeup contributes as much as one-third of the longevity formula. If you are fortunate to inherit the genetic code for a long life, you have a significant jumpstart on your path to longevity. In fact, half of all centenarians—people who live to 100 years of age or more—had parents, siblings or other relatives who also lived to 100.

But even if you aren't blessed with the magical genetic make-up, you can practice a lifestyle that promotes a long, healthy life. After all, if genetics is responsible for one-third of the longevity formula, most of the remaining two-thirds are behavioral. Most of your health is in your hands.

Happiness is one of those aspects over which you have at least some control. Depression can be quite serious and difficult to handle even with the best medications and counseling. But many of us simply don't take the time and effort to enjoy our many blessings. For this group, being happy is a choice.

"To your health and happiness!" is a toast that rings across the globe in every language. It is the universal wish for friends and family. Actually, it is a two-sided wish that works in tandem because we all know, without good health, it's tough to be happy. Both factors are vital in the formula for total well-being.

The oldest people in America are the happiest according to a study by Yang Yang, a University of Chicago sociologist. About 28,000 people aged 18 to 88 took part in the study. Yang Yang said that older people developed lower expectations and higher acceptance of others, increasing their appreciation of life. However, other studies also show that happier people live longer, so it is interesting to consider whether this particular group became happier as time went on or always were basically happy which led to their longevity.

The longer you live the more your circumstances change. Your attitude about it all is what makes the difference in your well-being. Taking everything in stride is good for your health. Proverbs 17:22 says, "A cheerful heart is a good medicine,/ but a downcast spirit dries up/ the bones." When you focus on your blessings, you feel more content with the many gifts around you. In their book, *Life Lessons,* Elisabeth Kubler-Ross and David Kessler say, "A grateful person is a powerful person, for gratitude generates power. All abundance is based on being grateful for what we have" (103).

Building a solid spiritual base also contributes towards longevity. Studies confirm that people with a strong faith do indeed live longer, healthier, and happier lives. One study showed nearly a quarter of the 100 Americans aged 99 years or older polled credited their faith as one of their secrets to longevity.

Spirituality's effect on one's health promotes not only longer living but better living as well. Spiritual people may even appear younger-looking, for when the spirit is strong, the body glows. A youthful, cheerful, and hopeful light is evident.

Of course, you can maintain all of the key factors and still suffer from disease or die prematurely. God's Will overrides everything. God may step in at any time and change or alter the plans you have for your future. Struggles, a sudden illness, or an accident may occur without any cause on your part, resulting in temporary or permanent disability or death. By the grace of God, you also may rarely be touched by difficulty or illness your entire life. Or you may recover completely from a fatal disease to the surprise of a medical professional—as well as yourself.

Every moment of our life is a God-given blessing. One
evening when I was out for dinner with family, restaurant
patrons were asked to sing "Happy Birthday" to a man
celebrating his 101st birthday. The spry "birthday boy" stood
up and thanked everyone for their kind wishes. When asked
what his secret to longevity was, he responded that he did not
have a secret. It was purely a gift which he greatly appreciated.

Impact of Spirituality on Aging

Studies show that the United States may be more of a spiritual
country than most think. At least this appears to be true for the
older generations. Research varies, but most reveal that about
75 percent or more of the senior population say their religion is
important to them. Half of all older Americans claim they
attend religious services weekly. Daily prayer also is
meaningful. Whether it is reading the Bible, praying the rosary,
or practicing other devotions, prayer is a part of most seniors'
daily lives.

For a clearer understanding of this topic, let's take a
moment to define the use of the words *faith, spirituality,* and
religion. These words are often misused or misunderstood. They
are closely related but do have some variances.

Faith is the acceptance and trust in a set of beliefs. The
Letter to the Hebrews describes faith in this way, "Now faith is
the assurance of things hoped for, the conviction of things not
seen" (Hebrews 11:1).

Religion and *spirituality* are often used interchangeably. But
there is a difference. *Religion* is usually understood to mean a
particular type of spirituality, such as Roman Catholic,
Lutheran, Eastern Orthodox, Buddhism, Hinduism, and so on.
Spirituality is the broader term indicating a quest for a fulfilled
life based on a set of beliefs and values. It is an expression of a
person's relation to a higher power. Through rituals, gestures,

and symbols, the connection to the source provides meaning to the life of that person.

For Christians, that set of beliefs and values are ones taught and exemplified by Jesus. It is the pursuit of holiness and Christ-like ways in addition to the dimension of the sacraments. *Catholic Dictionary* defines spirituality as, "The way an individual responds through grace to the call of Christ and His invitation to discipleship." It adds that conversion is always an element and continues, "Through Baptism and the other sacraments we are linked ever more deeply to our Savior and to all those redeemed by the Blood of His Cross."

William Reiser, SJ, puts this all together by writing in his book, *Looking for a God to Pray To* (2), "Spirituality refers to the unfolding, day by day, of that fundamental decision to become or remain a Christian which we make at baptism, repeat at confirmation, and renew each time we receive the Eucharist."

Spirituality and religious participation are known to increase with age. Duke University studies support this statement. These studies found that most hospitalized patients say their religion became more important to them as they grew older. In fact, faith is so important in later years that aging has been referred to as a "spiritual journey." On one survey, women aged 65 years and older ranked very high on their commitment to church attendance and service to others as well as the importance of their personal religious beliefs and biblical knowledge.

This growth in faith, or perhaps more correctly recognized as an evolution of faith, is due to many factors. Biblical and theological study, frequent attendance at religious services, presentations and discussion groups, and a variety of life experiences prompt an increasing interest in learning about one's faith. With age we realize more so than ever how much God's mark is on all aspects of the world.

It is not unusual for people in their 20s and 30s to say they are too busy to pray as often or for as long of a period of time as when they are in their later years. Time to pursue faith development competes with work and caring for a home and family as well as a host of extracurricular activities.

However, we may do well to root ourselves firmly in faith and work on strengthening it throughout our life. The earlier we start, the more we'll have when we need it most. We also will find that our faith grows when we lean on it in difficult situations. With the passing of time, nearly all of us will endure personal disappointment, loss, and illness. By the grace of God, our faith will not only see us through, it will increase and blossom more fully.

Perhaps we are privileged to have spiritual people who influenced us throughout our life. We are greatly blessed if we have parents who help to develop our faith when we are young, we continue to feed our faith over the years, and we allow the tough times to spiritually strengthen it further. Such a patchwork of spiritual challenges and influences and biblical study may become our security blanket. It is much like toning the body through daily physical exercises and then finding that it performs when challenged with agility and power.

This is not to say that we will not have moments of spiritual doubt. But for the most part, if we attend to our faith throughout our life, we will know the hand of God rests on our shoulder. We see God's presence, kindness, and love in all aspects of our life, good and bad. We recognize the abundance of blessings with which God has bestowed upon us and know we are never alone. Even on the darkest days, God, the saints, angels, and our heavenly mother are with us. They always have been and always will be.

This type of spiritual awareness is important for our longevity. Everything looks and feels differently through the lens of faith. When we believe and trust in a loving God we live and perceive our life in a special way. We are more aware of the power of God's grace and protection. We journey from a point of gratitude and we acknowledge our many blessings rather than becoming angry about what we don't have. We trust God to provide us with what we need, in God's perfect time, rather than what we think we should have, and when we think that we should have it.

Spirituality for Health

Spirituality is good for our health. There is a saying that our thoughts become our words, our words become our actions, and our actions become our reality. Negative, worrisome, or angry thoughts adversely affect the body. They pollute the body, mind, and spirit and manifest in pain and disability. Friends, family, and peers are affected by our foul actions and words as well.

In contrast, prayerful and peaceful thoughts alter the whole person and everyone around us in a positive way. Research finds that spirituality is associated with improved immune systems and fewer episodes of chronic inflammation. It also is known to lower rates of depression, a common condition in seniors. At least 25 percent of older adults suffer from depression, and that number increases significantly for those with physical illnesses.

Perhaps spirituality helps with these conditions because of the calming effect of prayer. Prayerful meditation can lower blood pressure and promote peacefulness in both mind and body. In addition, religion can be a strong deterrent to suicide (ASR.14). Older people with depression who are spiritual are less likely to intentionally harm themselves. A study in the September, 2008 *Journal of Affective Disorders* reported that suicide rates are lower among people who regularly attend religious services.

Spirituality relieves stress in difficult times. Throughout the struggles and heartaches of life, religion is the primary method by which a sizable portion of older Americans cope. As we age, we tend to turn toward our faith in the midst of turmoil.

Spirituality gives hope. When life gets tough, faithful people place their worries in God's hands. We pray, *Thy will be done,* and trust that God knows best and will take care of everything. All will be well. Our prayers remove at least a portion of the stress, and therefore, some of the damage stress does to the body. In a sense, we gain control by giving it up to our loving God. We are better able to continue our life journey one step at a time rather than be crippled by fear.

Some reports also suggest that how we handle the death of a loved one affects how long we will live. Using spirituality to cope with such a loss benefits our total being. This is particularly so when we are older and losing many friends, and most likely, in a more fragile physical state. Of course, it is much more effective to use our faith as a coping mechanism if a foundation is firmly in place before we need to stand on it. Those who do not have a spiritual base will find it difficult to draw support from something that hardly exists.

Widows adjust better to the loss of their spouse, and the many changes that result, if they are spiritual. One study cited in the book, *Religion and Coping* (conducted by McGloshen and OBryant), examined 226 widows between 60 and 89 years-old whose husbands recently passed away. They found the frequency of attendance at church workshops and services was the strongest predictor of how well the women handled their loss. The more services they attended, the better they did overall.

Most noteworthy is how spiritual people live. There is an accountability factor that overrides harmful lifestyle choices, or at the very least requires a moment of consideration before they act. The majority of centenarians (people who are 100 years of age or more) claim that they never were obese or smoked cigarettes, abused alcohol or drugs, or took dangerous risks. Spiritual people revere the body as a temple of the Holy Spirit. There is a responsibility to protect oneself and the spirit within from toxic substances or activities.

Spirituality also prompts forgiveness and reconciliation, which is physically and emotionally healthy. Catholics are required to acknowledge our failings and confess to a priest, thereby receiving forgiveness. We must be contrite—or sorrowful—for what we have done or failed to do. We then are given a penance—steps toward conversion, the turning away from sin and everything that offends God. These actions promote movement toward reconciliation with God and an uplifting of the weight of our sin.

As we ask God for forgiveness, it is necessary that we forgive those who offend us. Jesus is our perfect model. He pardoned his persecutors from the cross. God forgave all of our sins through Jesus' death. With one massive sweep, he wiped the entire slate clean.

In our society, this type of forgiveness rarely exists. We may "forgive" someone but still expect repayment for their actions against us. The perpetrator must pay a price whether it is monetarily, confinement, or even death.

Forgiveness doesn't mean condoning the hurtful actions or words, but we must forgive everything at all times. Scripture tells us this is so. Although complete forgiveness may not be easy, once it is done, the practice is a relief. It helps remove the burden of hurt and anger from our hearts and all the ill feelings that harm and weigh down our own well-being.

Alive in Our Faith

The magic formula to longevity isn't all that complicated. If we want a healthier, happier, and longer life, we must maintain a balanced diet, exercise program, optimistic outlook, and strong social network. These factors all play an important role.

In addition, revving up our spirituality becomes more and more critical as we age, because a faith-filled life improves all aspects of our well-being. Our spirituality helps us cope with the struggles and diminishes the destructive, accompanying stress. We benefit greatly by holding our faith in the center of our life and valuing each moment of every day.

Medical researchers define *successful aging* as an absence or low level of disease and disability. It is interesting to note that Christians who think of themselves as aging well are not necessarily the most physically healthy. They are the ones who are happy in spirit. They are spiritually strong and realize God's goodness and love in all that they see, hear, and do. As a result, they gather great joy from life.

There are several ways for seniors to build their faith. Practicing our personal prayers and devotions, participating in a faith community, serving and caring for fellow and older seniors, reaching for the Lord in our suffering and loss, and sharing our spiritual story with others are some of the ways we can strengthen our spirituality. If we are finding that this is difficult to do, we need only ask God to help us. Faith is a gift of the Holy Spirit. Pray for the Spirit to guide us toward healing the pain within and removing the obstacles that exist between us and God. Ask for the ability to grow stronger, healthier, and happier in the Spirit of the Lord.

O Holy Spirit, guide me through the obstacles that prevent me from loving you more fully. Help me to grow stronger, healthier, and happier in the Spirit of the Lord.

Strengthening Spirituality through Personal Devotions

Prayer is a fundamental language. Throughout history, the human response to helplessness has been the same—to implore a higher power to intervene on our behalf. Religion offers hope where there otherwise is none. When science, friends, and family run out of answers and possibilities, God responds. In times of need, we pray—which means to beg or implore—for divine assistance. We raise our hearts to God in adoration, thanksgiving, reparation, and petition.

Jesus' whole ministry was rooted in prayer. He gave instructions not only as to how we should pray but he also gave us the words to use. He said not to pray in such a way that brings attention to ourselves, but rather we should pray alone with our Father (Matthew 6:5-6). He taught the perfect prayer, the Our Father (Matthew 6:9-13). Jesus also said that victims should pray for their abusers (Luke 6:28).

We also learn about prayer from the Apostle Paul. Paul instructs the Thessalonians to pray without ceasing (1 5:17). More so, he teaches what to pray for. He says to ask God to make us worthy of his call and grant us the will to fulfill every work of faith that gives glory to Jesus (2 1:11-12).

Prayer is powerful. We see results in many little—and monumental—ways. We also find that the more we pray, the more we build on our relationship with God. As with any relationship, we are more comfortable and closer to those with whom we talk the most. So the more we talk with God, the closer we feel, which only makes us want to talk—or pray— increasingly more.

Pray Well—Be Well

When I was a child there was an elderly woman who I thought lived in the church. She could be found at any hour of the day kneeling in the front pew. Her rosary beads rattled incessantly before, during, and after Mass. A bulky sweater draped over her long dark dress and thick stockings all year round—in frigid cold and sweltering heat. The odor of urine permeated the air around her and kept parishioners at a distance.

Back then, I claimed a seat as far away from her as possible. Today, I pray for the woman and thank her for her fervent prayers. Whatever the intentions of her prayers, the world was a better place because of her. Her prayerful presence raised the parish and all those she touched in God's grace.

This devout woman illustrated the fact that we never are too old to pray or promote the faith. There is no retirement for a Christian. We are obligated to live the gospels, evangelize, spread the Good News of Jesus Christ, serve others by acting Christ-like, and communicate with God at every age.

We have so many reasons to pray. Our prayers may concentrate on the needs of the world and for strength and courage for the younger generations that they might fight for justice. Mostly, as we age, our prayers are for healing for ourselves and loved ones. Nearly 80 percent of Americans are said to believe in the power of prayer to improve illness (Moberg, 229).

Some researchers speculate that we merely receive a positive feeling from knowing people care enough to pray for us. It is that awareness that facilitates healing. They say that the person in need of prayer believes the prayers of others to be powerful and effective, and so they are. It is said that our healing is not a result of God's blessing but rather our own doing. Knowing there is prayer at work affects us physically.

For believers, this is far too limiting. We welcome prayers from friends and family because we know so much more is going on. We hand our prayers over to God fully believing that God hears us and responds. We trust that our prayers will be answered in God's time and God's way. All it takes is a good dose of patience.

Spiritual Development

There is comfort in knowing that in a quickly changing world, and in a time of life that requires detachment from possessions we worked a life-time to acquire but no longer need or have the ability to care for, God remains a constant, significant, and often growing aspect of our lives. God's steadfast love and mercy is infinite, always present within and around us. This does not mean that our relationship with God is stagnate. As with any healthy relationship, our prayer life and connection to the Lord evolves, changes, and grows.

Most faithful people say that their spirituality has deepened. It became more intimate with time. A life of joys and trials hopefully makes, rather than breaks, us and our relationship with God. Our everyday experiences and ongoing devotion feed, influence, and fuel our faith.

Many seniors also say that their prayer life is now more relaxed. This is due partly because they are less consumed with work. When they were younger, devotion was scheduled: an hour each weekend for church services or Mass, a weekly Holy Hour before the Blessed Sacrament. They prayed specific prayers in a particular way and at certain times. Hectic days left little opportunity for more than a quick morning prayer, blessings before a meal, and a prayer before bed.

With the passage of years, our spirituality often becomes more integral to our total being. Spiritual people move from a point of desire to one of gratitude, aware of the endless flow of blessings that we simply could not recognize when we were young. We gain an appreciation for the sacredness of every person, experience, and day. We see Christ working in all areas—the evidence of Christ in everything and everyone at all times.

Trusting in the ways of the Lord and accepting that God does know best is another development that occurs in faithful people over time. Painful events sometimes reveal themselves later in life as trigger points for growth and opportunity. We now see God's stamp on those times when it felt as if God abandoned us and every other stage of our life, no matter how difficult or painful the experience.

Another comfort is the **never**-changing Scripture. The Word of God is constant. We can depend on that. We also can continue to celebrate the Mass, sing sacred songs, and pray the prayers the same way we did when we were young (at least since the changes of Vatican II).

How We Pray

God didn't make any two of us absolutely identical, so it is likely that God doesn't expect our prayers to be identical either. We pray in countless ways. In word, song, art, and action throughout the centuries, we confidently send our pleas to the Lord. We speak personally from our hearts sending our worries and joys. And the list we pray for is endless.

Scientists have tried to measure the quality and effectiveness of prayer, but such an experiment is nearly impossible to conduct. Even if two individuals pray the exact same prayer in the exact same way, how can we know who prayed better or who had a more direct line of communication with God? Controlling such a study is difficult, to say the least.

We might say that if a prayer is favorably answered, we prayed well. But what actually accounted for someone's healing can't be determined. In addition, not getting what we prayed for does not mean that God didn't hear us. A "No" to a request also is an answer. The good Lord doesn't always reply in the way we hoped.

Studies show that results are seen in most cases where people prayed, regardless of whether or not the recipient is aware of prayers being sent to them. People who are prayed for heal quicker and more completely than those who are not. Patients don't even have to be in the near proximity of prayers. Nor do they have to belong to a particular faith or the same faith as the person praying for them to be affected.

Medical professionals are often in ideal situations to pray for the sick. Although most physicians say that they do in fact pray before surgery or while attending a patient, they rarely discuss this with those in their care. But regardless of whether or not the patient knows about the prayers, physicians and nurses do influence a patient's physiological responses. Their prayers are an important component in their patient's healing process.

When praying one thing is certain; all prayers made with good intentions are perfect prayers. If we pray for loved ones from a position of love, our prayers can only be powerful. Whether we pray alone or in a group, aloud or silently, our prayers move from our hearts to God's. And God hears all prayers no matter how simple or eloquent.

Prayer is a conversation with the divine. It is as individualized and unique as each one of us and the needs of the day. The Bible always offers us points to contemplate. As with my experience on the airplane, we often find that the verse we most need attracts our attention. We also may pray traditional prayers said for centuries, some of the more contemporary ones, or something straight from our heart. We may tell God, saints, or angels what we hold tightly within us in words we are comfortable using.

One of my models for praying is Vicka Ivankovic-Mijatovic, a visionary from Medjugorje, Bosnia-Herzegovina, who claims to see the Virgin Mary. I once had the privilege of standing before Vicka and watching her pray on the steps of her home. She prayed intently to Mary for at least 20 minutes, throughout which her face was exuberant. It was obvious that Vicka was holding an absolutely delightful conversation with a dear and loving friend. That is the image and experience I strive to emulate.

In a mini-survey administered while researching for this book, I found that middle-aged and senior people are practicing a wide range of devotions. The daily office, novenas, Divine Mercy and other chaplets, the rosary, reading Scripture, listening to sacred music, and contemplation were often said to be favorite forms of prayer. Responders also talked about the importance of Mass, the Eucharist, and Adoration before the Blessed Sacrament. They attend presentations by spiritual leaders and speakers and listen intently to homilies. Service work and participation in other forms of ministries are important as well.

One of the advantages of retirement is that our time is more flexible. Attending daily Mass is an uplifting way to start our day. It is a tremendous blessing if our church, or a neighboring one, offers weekday Masses and we are physically able to get there. The Mass nourishes us in so many ways. We have the Liturgy of the Word that gives us food for thought and contemplation and the Liturgy of the Eucharist to feed our bodies and souls with the body and blood of Jesus Christ. Jesus told us that the Eucharist is essential for our well-being. He said, "Those who eat my flesh and drink my blood have eternal life, and I will raise them up on the last day; for my flesh is true food and my blood is true drink" (John 6:54-55).

If daily Mass is not an option, an alternative is to start our day with 30 to 60 minutes of prayer and reflection. Beginning the morning in quiet, personal prayer sets a peaceful and joyful precedent for the rest of the day. We may meditate upon the daily Scripture readings, pray traditional prayers, or speak informally to God. Some days one form of prayer may feel more right than another. The choice is ours.

We find so many answers and so much comfort from reading the Scriptures. As we saw earlier, Psalm 118 alone can be our daily mantra. And there is more to this rich and complex psalm than the verse, "This is the day the Lord has made. Let us rejoice and be glad in it." The psalm was written in thanksgiving and originally sung at a victory procession. Ancient people confidently asked God for help when they were threatened, and God rescued them. The psalm gives thanks for the Lord's goodness and steadfast love. It instructs us to put our faith in the Lord rather than earthly princes. Place our trust in God's strength, might, and salvation, the psalm recommends. It also blesses those who come in the name of the Lord.

Verse 22 reads, "The stone that the builders rejected/ has become the chief cornerstone," and is referenced several times in the New Testament. The stone is often believed to refer not only to the foundation of the temple but to the death and resurrection of Christ as well. Jesus is the stone that was rejected.

Jesus himself quotes this verse when he asks the chief priests and elders in the temple, "Have you never read in the scriptures;/the stone that the builders rejected/has become the cornerstone;/this was the Lord's doing,/ and it is amazing in our eyes'?" (Matthew 21:42). Jesus continues saying that the one who falls on this stone will be broken to pieces; and it will crush anyone on whom it falls. (See Romans 9:33, 1 Peter 2:7, and Acts 4:11 for further New Testament references to this Old Testament passage.)

Such profound messages can be found in the other psalms as well. The full collection of 150 psalms is called the Psalter, which comes from the Greek word, *Psalterion*, a stringed instrument. The Hebrew name is *tehillim*, which means hymns or songs. Often prompted by events in Israel's history, the psalms were composed in lovely, digestible phrases for singing at liturgical worship. David, the royal harpist and singer, is attributed with writing at least 73 of them, although that can be debated because authorship was often given to a respected professional in the field.

Most of the psalms are lamentations and begin with a cry for help. Psalm 118 is considered a Royal Psalm, a royal thanksgiving. Others include Wisdom, Liturgical, and Historical Psalms. The exact dates that they were written are unknown. Some are thought to date back as early as 1000 B.C.

The power of the psalms to inspire and promote greater devotion was so important in the early church that Irish monks recited all of them every day. However, this practice did pose some challenges. Many monks were illiterate and could not read the Psalter. Others could not afford to own a copy, and memorizing all 150 in their entirety was nearly impossible. These obstacles resulted in the development of the rosary around the year 1096.

As an alternate practice the monks began reciting 150 Our Fathers, the prayer Jesus taught and that is found in Scripture. The monks kept count by following knots or beads tied on a string. They soon placed a bead separating each of the five groups of ten. Our Fathers were prayed and various Scripture verses were meditated upon the single beads. Hail Marys, which draw from the Annunciation and Visitation of Mary to her cousin Elizabeth as found in the Gospel of Luke (1:28, 1:42), were recited on those beads and clustered in decades. When praying the rosary three times around with the original three sets of mysteries, the total Hail Mary's equaled the number of psalms in the Psalter.

The rosary evolved with the meditation on various Scriptures that highlight specific events in the life, death, and glory of Jesus. These key points are now known as Mysteries. For about 500 years there were three sets of Mysteries—the Joyful, Sorrowful, and Glorious. In 2002 Pope John Paul II proposed a fourth set, called the Luminous

Mysteries, also known as the Mysteries of Light, which focus on Jesus' ministry.

Seniors who grew up praying the rosary still find this form of prayer gives great comfort. The rosary is one of my favorite forms of prayer because it encourages peacefulness and a higher level of compassion for those I pray for, even those who hurt me. Younger generations with less exposure to the rosary also will find it fulfilling. Many who replied to my questionnaire said they enjoyed meditation and contemplation, which can be prompted by praying the rosary. (If you are not confident in praying the rosary, pick up a copy of my book, *The Rosary Prayer by Prayer*. You can pray the rosary easily with this book by following page after page.)

The rosary's evolution reveals the impact of the psalms on personal devotion, as well as their ongoing incorporation in the liturgy. From ancient times to the present, the psalms have offered comfort and reassurance in God's love and mercy. We cry out to God as we sing, "The LORD is my light and my/ salvation;/ whom shall I fear"(27:1); "The LORD is my shepherd, I shall not/ want" (23:1), and "My refuge and/ my fortress;/ my God, in whom I trust" (91:2). With the recitation of the psalms, God hears our praise, joy, tears, and sorrows.

We live in precarious times. If we're not struggling with a major obstacle, someone close to us is. Unemployment and underemployment jeopardize not only many people's financial security but their housing, food supply, medical care, education, and future plans as well. Natural disasters around the world bring devastating results. And many of us seem to suffer from some type of health issue.

Repose can be found by reading the psalms as well as the other rich books of the Bible. Be open to their messages and know that God continues to speak through them. Even in the midst of our greatest sadness or struggles, God is with us.

We also can seek inspiration and direction from spiritual books written by a variety of authors. These books tap into the wide range of topics within the genre of spirituality. We can

read about our religion, holy people who have shown us how
to live more fully in Christ and how to apply faith to our daily
lives. We don't even have to leave our home to find these
books. If we can't make it out to our local bookstore, gift shop,
or library, we can phone in or order them online. Today we
also have the option of downloading books and reading them
on e-readers such as the Kindle, tablet, or cell phone.

Saints for Support

Prayer in numbers is powerful, and we never have to pray
alone. In addition to soliciting prayers from living friends and
family as we are instructed to do in Scripture (James 5:14), we
can pray to—which actually means in most cases to pray
with—our spiritual friends. In addition to praying to God—the
Father, Son, and Holy Spirit—we can ask saints and angels to
join us in prayer. Our holy mother, Mary, especially as Our
Lady of Lourdes when we are ill, is waiting to hear from us.
Guardian angels also remain close, ready to assist.

We may call on a favorite saint. The Catholic Church
believes saints intercede on our behalf if something seems
impossible. They pray with the petitioner and ask God for
a miracle.

The Catholic Church investigates miracles in connection
with the canonizations of saints. Following the candidate's
death, two miracles must be attributed to the candidate's
intervention in order for the candidate to be approved for
sainthood (with the exception of martyrs). Most of the
resulting miracles incorporate physical healings. Clergy,
medical professionals, and laity sit on panels that scrutinize
and deliberate over every detail of the potential saint's life
and works, the so-called miracle, and the recipient of the
miracle. No natural or medical explanation may be found for
the sudden and complete cure. Studies may continue for

generations before concluding with a final decision to bring the candidate before the Holy Father for papal approval.

Because of the extent of "proof" needed, most cases are not approved. Those that are, allow us to trust that prayer does work. God hears us in our pain and illness and heals in astounding ways on behalf of our own prayers and those of our friends who are living and deceased. The approval of the Church also acknowledges the dependability of the saint to carry our prayers to God.

The purpose of canonizing saints is not to honor the holy person but rather to provide the faithful community with role models. These saints are recognized as patrons of certain causes. We pray to them—or rather ask them to pray for and with us. Scripture instructs us to petition prayer from one another (Thessalonians 2 3:1-2). Saints were human persons who lived and suffered as we do. Their prayers are especially beneficial because of their close association to God and complete understanding of the perils of human life.

Many of these saints are patrons of causes such as aging, illness, suffering, and death. Mary the mother of Jesus is our greatest saint. People worldwide have prayed to her since she walked this earth. Pilgrims pay special honor to her by traveling to a shrine in her name, especially when in need of physical healing. The personal sacrifice of time and money prove how confident the pilgrims are in seeking favorable answers to their prayers. Millions visit these sites each year. The shrine in Lourdes, France, is particularly recognized for miraculous healings. But we don't have to travel to Lourdes or any shrine for Mary to hear and respond to our call for help. Our Holy Mother listens to all and joins us in our prayers whenever and wherever we ask.

A saint considered predominantly interested in the conditions of aging is Saint Apollonia. In her old age, Appolonia was burned to death for her faith. Other saints from whom seniors may want to solicit prayers include Saint Anthony of Padua, the patron of the elderly; Saint Alphonsus

Marie Liguori, bishop and father of the Church who suffered from crippling rheumatism; Saint Giles, the Abbot, patron saint of people with disabilities; and St. Jude the Apostle, the patron of impossible causes.

Saint Peregrine Laziosi (1260-1345) is the patron saint of persons suffering from cancer, AIDS, and other serious diseases. Peregrine practiced what is known as "dream prayer." This is prayer that takes place while sleeping. Some think it is the most effective form of prayer because we have fewer distractions or inhibitions when we sleep.

During his life here on earth, Peregrine developed a painful cancer in his foot. The evening before a scheduled amputation, he prayed earnestly through the night. After falling asleep he had a vision of the crucified Jesus leaving the cross and touching his foot. Peregrine awoke to find the cancer completely vanished. He lived 20 years after the vision.

Saint Theodora (also known as Saint Mother Theodore Guérin) is another saint who may be called upon by those who suffer with cancer. Canonized in 2006, she is the eighth American to be recognized as a saint. Saint Theodora founded the American order of the Sisters of Providence in Indiana and Saint Mary-of-the-Woods College.

The first miracle after her death was granted to one of the sisters in her order, Sister Mary Theodosia. The sister was cured from cancer as well as a disability that resulted from a previous surgery. Saint Theodora also is known to have assisted a man suffering from a serious vision problem. That was the second miracle recognized for her canonization. So we may call on her for prayers when a loved one is struggling with diseases or conditions of the eyes.

In addition to praying for the wellness of friends, family, and ourselves, we might consider praying for our health providers. Saint Camillus de Lellis, the patron of nurses, founded the Ministers of the Sick (the Camellians). Camillus ministered in Rome and Naples and sent members of his order to assist the wounded troops in Hungary and Croatia. We also have patron saints for caregivers, such as Saint Aloysius Gozaga who cared for patients suffering from the plague at great risk to his own health. (You can find more interesting saints for seniors in the appendix of this book.)

Leaning on Faith

Maintaining our spiritual health is one key to a happy, healthy, and long life. Spiritual people navigate through the challenges of aging on the wings of faith. Our trust in God allows us to sail through the tough times more easily by lightening the weight of anxieties and fears. Once we give our troubles up to God, we don't need to worry about them anymore. If we want assistance, saints and angels are ready and willing to help us.

Faith also encourages the recognition of the many blessings and joys that surround us every day. Even in the worst of times, we have so many gifts for which to be thankful. Looking to the positive, rather than dwelling on the negative, is the healthiest choice. It is a constructive practice that benefits our entire self.

We are holistic beings—which comes from the Greek word *holos*, meaning all-encompassing. Scientists and theologians agree that an interconnection between body, mind, and spirit does exist. When one aspect of our being is weakened, the others suffer. Strengthen one and the others benefit as well.

Maintaining such a balance is necessary in caring for the total person. But this is not always possible. As we age, the breakdown of the body strains the mind and sometimes, the spirit as well. On the other hand, our entire self benefits when we nourish the soul. When the spirit is lifted, joy resonates through our body.

Faith is not unchanging. It fluctuates, dips, and soars with life's ups and downs. Our spirit needs daily attention, beginning with private, personal prayer time, to sustain the trials experienced by the whole body. In order to be spiritually

strong each moment of every day until our last breath, we must
continuously nurture and nourish it. We must pray—
connecting and communicating with God every moment of
every day.

The benefits of prayer are endless, as are the ways in which
we can pray. Add the names of family, friends and fellow
parishioners to our prayer list and ask them to include our
name on theirs. Join or form a prayer group or Bible study. As
we pray for other members, they will pray for us, all members
of one Body of Christ.

Here I am Lord, your faithful, loving servant.
I place my many worries before you.
Thank you for hearing my prayers.

Strengthening Spirituality
Through the
Faith Community

Life is about relationships—our relationship with God and with humanity. We are an interconnected world-wide community, and we have profound effects on one another. The power to heal heartache and raise the consciousness of the world through love and compassion lies within us all. This can be done with the simplest gesture: smile at someone and they smile back.

Research shows a direct correlation between the number of people in our circle of friends and our well-being. The larger our social support system, the lower our mortality rate. It is as if loved ones form a protective mesh, a safety net of sorts, which softens the blows and enhances the joys of life. They are God-given gifts. We should lean on and enjoy the people in our lives, and help them when they are in need.

It is easier than ever to make friends with people all over the world. We can meet and mingle via Internet blogs, websites, social networks, and email. We can become a part of any number of small communities, connecting with people of different nationalities, cultures, and ideas.

However, there is a major drawback to this method. Computer friendships lack physical contact. These new means of communication are intangible. They cannot give us the components of eye contact or body language, or the smells, sounds, and feel of another person. These avenues also promote a false sense of invulnerability. They are a platform on which to voice our thoughts and opinions behind the mask and shield of the computer. In this way we are less likely to sensor the words we spew from the keyboard—words that have a lasting effect and may be imprinted in cyberspace for an unlimited period of time.

In contrast, words that are spoken in the presence of another person have an accountability factor. We instantly see the effect of our words. We are called out on the accuracy or hurtfulness of our comments. We also see the impact of kindness, how it continues to ripple out from the recipient to their surrounding circle of friends and relatives.

Personal contact is one of the many benefits of belonging to a church. The social network of a parish provides a group of spiritually like-minded people that we can socialize with, which is an essential component for well-being. It offers the physical presence of people with whom we can share coffee, friendship, and prayer. Here we gain peers who care and pray for one another, feeding our souls as well as our minds and bodies.

Parishioners offer a sounding board to talk to about our problems and anxieties. They can also help relieve stress. Together, we acknowledge and celebrate accomplishments, share aspirations and heartaches, raise each other's self-esteem, and nurse the wounds of life. We also continue to shape our spiritual identity through the Word, sacraments, traditions, rituals, and symbols of our faith.

Physical Accommodations in the Church

Unfortunately, at a time when the church community and experience is critically needed, many senior members encounter obstacles. In order to receive the gifts of a church, parishioners must be able to physically get there. Many are unable to attend services and other related activities as often as they'd like. Physical disabilities and lack of transportation deny them Christian companionship and nourishment.

Once at the church, parishioners also need access to the building. Activities such as climbing stairs, clearly hearing a sermon, and reading small print in prayer books become difficult with age. So much of the prayer experience is lost if the service cannot be heard or seen. It is essential for the liturgical ministers to devote some of their attention to this.

Easy access to public buildings is fairly commonplace today. Some accommodations are mandated by law. But at the very least, one entrance to the church should be wheel chair and walker accessible in addition to providing open spaces within to park mobility aides. An elevator to meeting rooms on other floors also is helpful for young mothers with strollers as well as elderly members. Large-print editions of Bibles, hymnals, and prayer books as well as the installation of an adequate sound system and personal hearing devices are greatly appreciated.

In addition, an emergency intervention plan should be considered. There are likely to be occasions when paramedics may be called during a service. Emergency crews need easy access to a parishioner in crisis.

Until medical help arrives, many churches and other public buildings have installed at least one Automated External Defibrillator in the event a member suffers a heart attack. Known as an AED, this portable electronic device diagnoses cardiac arrhythmias of ventricular fibrillation and ventricular tachycardia. The AEDs treat the conditions through defibrillation which stops the arrhythmia and helps reestablish an effective rhythm. Some parishioners should be trained with these, but the equipment also comes with instructions. We can do the most good by maintaining a sense of awareness and being ready to react in the event one of our seniors needs help.

Extending warm greetings when entering the church also is important. Even with other parishioners surrounding them in the pews, seniors can feel quite alone. Welcoming those around us is a small gesture that promotes a sense of inclusion and worth.

This is particularly true for seniors who may have relocated to a new church after belonging somewhere else for many years. The contrast of once sitting with friends and family and knowing almost everyone around them to sitting amongst strangers can be very sad and lonely. Familiar faces and friendly handshakes are sorely missed. A little gesture of kindness can make all the difference.

I often am alone in church. Looking around at all the families sometimes makes me lonesome for when my young children came with me. My solution is to sit with a senior who also is alone. We have the company of one another and someone to wish "Peace be with you" until the other people around us finish greeting their loved ones.

For those who are too ill or disabled to attend any church service, some opportunity for communal prayer is available through Christian radio and television shows, newspapers, magazines, and books. Many Christians without physical disabilities also tune in. For the homebound, the programming offers the main or only means of "attending" service or receiving spiritual information.

Serving Seniors in the Church

For some denominations, especially Catholics, the Mass and Eucharist are the most important sources of spiritual nourishment. Bible studies, seminars, presentations, and retreats also are highly valued. Clergy and women of local religious communities who provide personal spiritual direction are important to members as well.

Bingo, coffee hours, and bus outings top the list of church-sponsored activities for senior members. Social outlets build community and maintain the overall health of the church. They keep us playful and provide the opportunity of fun and camaraderie. Other social activities include meals, shopping, exercise classes, health seminars and screenings, financial guidance, grief counseling, substance abuse recovery meetings, caregiver support, nutrition classes, and adult day care.

And yet, many parishioners want more from their parish. Although these programs are important, many parishes do not provide enough spiritual development and direction specifically designed for seniors. Faith development for midlife and older adults is critical for the transformation of our aging world. We need a selection of programs and services targeted toward seniors and their caregivers on aging, dying, and death.

In our later years, we turn our attention inward and analyze our relationship with God. We, the faithful, search for meaning in our earthly life and question our readiness for our eternal life with God. Theological classes for seniors provide the knowledge we need to contemplate and understand what we must do now and what we might expect as we move from this world to the next. Such classes provide a setting to discuss our deepest thoughts and share our questions with our peers.

The last conversation I had with my 37 year-old cousin, Bridget, who was dying from cancer, dealt with death and dying. We talked about her crossing over into the next life and what her soulful existence might be like after that. She said she was grateful for the conversation and opportunity to discuss what weighed heavy on her mind. Few people wanted to talk about it with her, she said. The thought of death or losing our Bridget made them too uncomfortable.

Some seniors also have requested traditions or milestones to continue to be honored in later years. Life is a gift to be celebrated at all ages. Many seniors have not been recognized in the church for several decades. Masses for special birthdays or simply for everyone over 65 would show our elders that they are a valued dimension of our family of faith. In addition, May crownings and festivals for favorite saints are uplifting ways to remember the celebrations of years gone by.

The senior adult ministries, as with all solid programming, must be organized and consistent. Form and content are vital considerations when planning events and should include curricula specifically for senior adults. Quality resources and training support for ministry leaders is essential. Facilitators must be educated and informed. Senior programs need to appeal to the vast differences between people over 65 years of age who span several decades and generations. The result of such programming, if successful, would be motivational and informative. It also would fire the spirit of evangelization and encourage carrying the message of Christ to others.

A concern raised by organizers of senior programming is that attendance is often low at these events. This may be due to the logistics of transporting aging participants, so it is helpful to have transportation available. Seniors who can drive might invite other members to ride with them.

A personal invitation is also helpful. Sometimes we need a hand to reach out and take us along. Encouraging other seniors to attend and welcoming them into the fold can be the push they need to cross the threshold of shared faith and find friendship. We shouldn't be discouraged if our offer is turned down multiple times. We never know when the timing might be perfect for someone to finally take the leap with us.

Also, programs are more meaningful when they are relational and reciprocal. If we are involved in senior programming, we must encourage other seniors to participate and serve in the planning and presentation. Involving seniors in the development of these events increases the likelihood the programs will interest them—and that they'll attend.

Pastoral Care for Seniors

Our Judaic roots mandate the care of widows and that we honor our elders. Scripture provides certain age-specific rituals and responsibilities, including the visitation of the sick and dying. We begin following these instructions by reaching out to our own family, friends, and fellow parishioners.

The church can be, and often is, a source of assistance. Senior adults may reach out to their clergy for help, and therefore, priests must be prepared to respond personally or by making informed referrals. The parish office staff must have guidelines to follow as well. Pastoral care is most beneficial when it is available at all times, not only at the point of death when a person's needs are obvious.

First and foremost, a person's basic physical needs must be met. If we are approached by a parishioner seeking help we might ask if they are receiving necessary medical care, food, and shelter. They also may want an advocate to guide them through health care, living assistance, and financial questions. Spiritual needs may be helped by administering communion, spiritual counseling, and prayer. Most often we will not personally provide what the senior needs but rather act as a liaison and direct them to the appropriate parish ministry or social service group.

Many churches have a nurse on staff. This is a fabulous resource for whole-body ministry that disseminates information, provides health screenings, and prompts discussions on age-related spiritual concerns. Parish nurses are in positions to distribute educational materials. Some may be transmitted through church bulletins, local and diocesan newspapers, and parish mailings. Nurses also may offer screenings for blood pressure and cholesterol at nominal fees after Sunday services.

So many senior adults are underinsured. They suffer chronic illness but have little resources to expend on the high cost of health-care. Many did not receive adequate health-care in their younger years which might have prevented later illness. Help with these issues is invaluable. Some parish nurses are available for these services as well.

Grief support and counseling are also important services for seniors. Perhaps it seems a bit ridiculous to point out that the majority of deaths in our society occur in older people. But this illustrates the fact that seniors are continuously leaving this earth. Losing so many friends and relatives at a seemingly rapid pace, while contemplating our own illness and death, can be depressing and bring on feelings of loneliness.

For those of us who do not feel our death or that of a loved one will occur for some time, the future appears open to opportunities. We can enjoy planning activities and looking forward to them. We have hope when things aren't perfect that they will be in the future. For those whose death appears near, that particular sense of hope and joy is more fragile. A parish nurse, pastoral counselor, and programs dedicated to grieving can facilitate a healthy response to so much loss.

We also must bring the parish community to the home-bound in a small but important way. Those who are temporarily or permanently unable to attend services, long for the faith community. Remembering those seniors who are restricted to their homes or assisted living facilities means so much to them. If their homes reside within the parish, they are a part of the parish family and must be recognized as such.

One of the greatest gifts we can give our seniors is our presence. Our participation in their lives can make a difference in their happiness and overall well-being. Administering to their spiritual needs brings affirmation. It acknowledges them as a significant part of the Christian community. Young people will find that the ministry of serving the elderly results in tremendous gain on several levels.

There are many ways we might assist our seniors. Able-bodied members help by driving them to services as often as possible. They also can call on the homebound for short visits in person or over the phone. Lay ministers, women religious, priests, and deacons also touch our seniors personally and spiritually. By fulfilling a spiritual hunger with the serving of the Eucharist and prayer we also offer ourselves as a companion in Christ. We are there to listen and offer friendship to someone who may have few remaining peers.

Pray with them, read Scripture, or sing familiar hymns. We may need to shorten services so as not to tax our fellow parishioners too much. But even someone seemingly detached from this world may find comfort from Mass and other services because they are experienced through multiple senses. The Catholic faith is rich in symbolism, and those symbols are powerful triggers for all of us including people suffering physical and cognitive disabilities.

Someone may be speechless as a result of a stroke but can experience the religious activities through other senses, reminding them of God's love. The familiarity of the sounds, scents, and movements of the rituals can promote a deep level of devotion or spiritual calmness. A worshiper may not comprehend the Scripture reading or sermon and yet be spiritually moved by the readings, music, aroma of incense, bells ringing, or touch of a blessing. The rituals spark memories and emotions enjoyed in earlier years.

Sending cheerful notes also benefits those we cannot see. Include bulletins and newsletters in the mailings in the event the parishioner may be physically able to attend a service in the future. The bulletins keep them informed and provide a personal invitation acknowledging that they remain an important part of the faith community.

And if we are a senior in need of support or companionship, we may talk to our pastor about ways younger or healthier members may help us. Perhaps no one is aware of our need. Asking for assistance provides others with opportunities to be Christ to us. Both we and our fellow parishioner have much to gain by the relationship.

Senior Roles in the Faith Community

As society ages, so will the population within the church. Statistics are showing that more than half of the membership in mainline Protestant churches is 50 years of age or older.

Catholic churches are not quite that extreme, but the membership in most parishes is growing proportionately older.

This situation of aging churches leads to a statement heard periodically: if a parish's congregation consists primarily of older adults, the parish is dying. Such a remark is demeaning and far from the truth. In fact, the senior population is a tremendous resource, albeit largely untapped, that can play an important role in a dynamic church.

Two questions arise in any relationship and so also apply to our membership in the Christian community. We selfishly ask first how the other party serves us (which is the opposite of servitude in the way that Christ taught). We then must also ask how we may serve. And a good many of the seniors in the church do indeed wish to give of themselves.

The problem is that although the senior population is substantial, it can be quite invisible in a congregation. This is due in part because the remaining parish is unaware of their abilities and desires to assist with parish needs. As stated earlier, seniors struggle with transportation and health issues that limit their ability to attend services, meetings, and gatherings. There also is the tendency to intentionally remain in the background. Many seniors are reluctant to participate in existing programs because they feel they have little to offer, that they are inadequate, old-fashioned, and unneeded.

This is an unfortunate waste of resources from a diverse segment of the congregation. Plenty of senior parishioners are healthy, able-bodied, and willing to contribute toward the many ministries of the church, serving where others do not have the time or ability to do so. This extensive group possesses a variety of talents, gifts, capabilities, creativity, and wisdom. They are a rich source of role models and mentors; storytellers and historians; evangelists and catechists; and liturgical volunteers. They also include several generations and the personal and generational experiences that left their mark. This makes the senior membership an experienced, knowledgeable, and powerful asset to the faith community with time to serve.

Your parish may be similar to mine in that it offers a long list of ministries in which to can get involved. In my church community, the Cana Guild assists with weddings; the Saint Catherine Guild prepares and delivers meals for families in emergency situations; and the Holy Spirit Guild provides white baptismal bibs and helps out at baptisms. For those who prefer to serve from home, parishioners can pray for expectant parents and their babies or those longing to become pregnant or adopt as well as parents grieving a miscarriage, stillbirth, or the death of an infant. For members who want to do something more physical, we have the Friendship Garden, a garden that supplements food for our church food pantry.

Check the ministries your parish sponsors to see which ones appeal to your abilities and talents. If you are a senior, be open and discerning as to how God wishes to use you at this point in your life. God calls disciples of all ages. You may be quite surprised at what you find yourself doing.

Scripture offers many vivid examples of older individuals asked by God to fulfill tasks one might think could only be accomplished by the young. As Joshua learned, we are never too old for the Lord to assign a major undertaking. Joshua was quite advanced in years when the Lord told him to divide the land for an inheritance to the nine tribes and the half tribe of Manesseh (Joshua 14:1). Moses was 80 years-old when he spoke to the pharaoh (Exodus 7:7). Abraham was more than 100 years old when God put him in charge of a multitude of nations (Genesis 17:15). After never having a child her whole life, Sarah became a mother in later years (Genesis 17:17). And Anna, the holy prophet, was one of the few people who saw Jesus for whom he was. She was "at a great age" yet fully capable of recognizing what others could not—that the infant Jesus was the long awaited Messiah (Luke 2:36).

Serving the needs of the parish benefits the seniors who serve as well as the church. One of the keys to longevity is having a purpose. For the bulk of our lives, work prompts that incentive. It is where 90 percent of our daily attention is focused. The drawback here is that it becomes the double-edged sword, one side being an asset to longevity and the other prompting a sense of loss and unworthiness when our work no longer exists.

In our senior years, rather than limiting our self only as a *former* carpenter, doctor, teacher, manager, or customer service rep, we must look deeper within to find the essence of our being. Senior years often allow opportunities for personal development. Goals long put on hold may finally be explored. It's not unusual for older adults to return to school and venture into new careers at a time when others are ending theirs.

If retirement funds are adequate, we may delve into work with little or no financial return but that promotes the greater good. Examples include participating in programs that raise literacy or serve people who are poor, hungry, or homeless. These ministries serve people in need as well as offer a valuable "reason to get up in the morning." They are ways in which we can invest in building other people.

We Christians also gain much of our identity from our faith, so this is a great time for personal and spiritual development. The Holy Spirit blesses us with a unique package of talents, some that may be easier to develop later in life. These gifts can be utilized within and through the church. Join a Bible study group or take a class offered by the diocese. Since Christians develop much of our sense of self from our faith, devoting more time to activities in the church can help to redefine our new sense of identity and purpose. We may increase our commitment with other parishioners and participate in liturgical services or ministerial or charitable work.

Women's Roles in the Church

There are more women than men in the United States. In the segment of the population who are 85 and older, that ratio is two to one. These numbers are reflected in the church, and yet women are limited to the roles in which to serve, particularly in some Christian denominations, including Catholic. This continues to be a point of contention for some women.

Liberation Theology is a movement that emerged from Latin America and emphasizes the Christian commitment to the suffering of the politically and economically oppressed. Feminist Theology is considered a branch of this movement because it seeks justice for women and the alleviation of the oppression felt by many. Feminist Theology is the belief that women are entitled to the same rights and privileges in the Church as men. According to this position, the existing patriarchal system wrongfully excludes women from participating in a Church that belongs to everyone equally, regardless of gender.

Women's views on this topic vary greatly. Some are completely satisfied or prefer only minor changes. Others believe there should be absolutely no gender-based differences in the Church. They believe in using inclusive language for humans as well as for the images and names for God. In addition, feminists believe that women should be allowed liturgical leadership and participation in decision making in all areas of church governance. They see a Church in need of capable and appropriate candidates for priesthood, and are willing and able to answer the call. There are senior women who want the option to enter the priesthood or deaconate as so many older men are doing today.

Elizabeth Johnson writes in *She Who Is*, "Women are equally created in the image and likeness of God, equally redeemed by Christ, equally sanctified by the Holy Spirit." She adds that women also are equally involved in the tragedy of sin, called to evangelize, and destined for eternal life with God.

An argument against women's right to ordination in some denominations stem from Jesus' choice of apostles. There is no doubt that the apostles were men. But if we are to limit candidates only to those like Jesus selected, some feel limitations should apply to several areas. The church then could only choose ones of the same ethnicity, professions, physical characteristics, ages and so on as seen in the apostles.

Feminists feel that since Jesus' entire ministry was based on social justice, he would be open to women serving the Church in all capacities. More specifically, he treated women with respect and kindness in a time when women had little voice or power over their own well-being much less their home or community. Many women even participated in Jesus' ministry and were recipients of miraculous blessings. This discipleship of women continued well into the early Church.

Seniors on the Outskirts

As we age, the struggle to find our place in the faith community, as well as society as a whole, becomes even more complicated and emotional when we are a member of a minority group. Our Church consists of a kaleidoscope of ethnicity and lifestyles that are reflected in our liturgy and parish activities. Honoring everyone's God-given differences is our Christian obligation.

Seniors who are Native American, African American, or Latino encounter an array of additional challenges, especially in areas of economics and education. If educational and employment opportunities were limited in earlier years, the likelihood of illness and poverty increases in senior years. For example, blood pressure and cholesterol levels are commonly higher among African Americans. These conditions lead to a higher probability of Alzheimer's and vascular dementia in addition to other physical disabilities, all of which prevent full participation in church activities and services.

Our American Christian churches are moving from memberships that consisted predominately of people of European descent to a more global mix. Approximately one-third of the U.S. population is Latino. As the Latino percentage of the U.S. population increases, so does the Latino population in the Church. Many people of Eastern Indian and African descent are entering our churches in America in growing numbers as well. We also find quite a diversity of cultures in churches in the Hawaiian Islands, which includes people of Hawaiian, Pilipino, Tongan, Chinese, Korean, Japanese, and Portuguese descent.

Such a variety of cultures presents us with an opportunity to grow spiritually in unprecedented ways. We have much to learn from one another. But some older people have difficulty in accepting the unfamiliar. It may be challenging to pray comfortably in a new parish if relocation is necessary or even in our own parish should the population of the neighborhood lean toward a different incoming culture and its unknown music and traditions.

Another difference we find in our parish is that of lifestyle. Estimates show about 3 million people over the age of 55 are classified as LGBT—lesbian, gay, bisexual, or transgender. That number is projected to increase to nearly 4 million over the next 10 years. And most certainly, whether we are aware or not, many of these people practice their faith alongside of us in the pew. Most denominations declare homosexual acts to be sinful. As a result, members who are actively homosexual may be discriminated against, shunned, or completely alienated from the church. They then are crippled in practicing their faith.

Whatever your views on gender, lifestyle, race, or cultural differences, we must remember that we will be judged in the same way that we judge others (Matthew 7:1-2). Jesus reached out to all people, especially those marginalized by society. He befriended all the lepers of his society including women, children, tax collectors, and the sick, so our objective must be to treat everyone in the faith community with respect. We are to love our neighbors as ourselves (Matthew 22:39) in the way that Jesus did.

Serving and Being Served within the Faith Community

Participating in a church community can be a source of
support, inspiration, and education and a means in which to
serve those in need. Here we often find access to age-specific
information and peers that help cultivate our faith. Through
service and the humbling experience of being served, we grow
closer to the Lord.

There are so many ways in which this can be done. In
addition to attending regular and special services, we can
participate in or organize presentations and forums for
discussions specifically targeted toward seniors. We can join
forces in praying for the needs of the parish and the world. We
also can allow others to come to our aide, especially in a
spiritual way. Volunteer to teach catechism classes, share the
Eucharist with those who are homebound, or usher and
welcome fellow parishioners into the church. We also may
invite parishioners to add our name to their prayer list or come
to our home for short visits.

A church parish is a community in faith, a family that
consists of many diverse and interesting personalities. Be open
to seeing Christ within even those whom we do not
understand. In the senior years when we need assistance from
others to help with our physical, mental, emotional, and
spiritual concerns of aging, tolerance is imperative. We cannot
expect to be treated with respect and dignity if we do not grant
the same to our fellow human beings.

Lord, make me an instrument of peace and service.
Help me to share and grow in faith with
all of my brothers and sisters in Christ.

Strengthening Spirituality Through Caregiving

One of Jesus' last concerns before dying on the cross was for his mother. In keeping with the Fourth Commandment (Exodus 20:12), he honored her until his final breath. Jesus entrusted her to his beloved friend, John, knowing the disciple would care for her as if she was his own mother (John 19:26-27).

When we care for our seniors, we are to do so in the way that Saint John did. It is as if Jesus personally places his loved one in our care. The recipient of care is no stranger but rather a child of God, our brother or sister in Christ. We are to treat the recipient as we would if she was Jesus' Mother.

We are biblically responsible for ensuring the well-being of the young and the old. Saint Paul had a special concern for orphans and widows (James 1:27). Although men are providing care more often than previous generations, women typically are the ones to do this. According to statistics gathered by the organization, OWL, nearly 80 percent of family caregivers are women. The Caregiver Alliance estimates this number is closer to 90 percent.

In addition to children, which may or may not be our own, we probably have, are, or will care for an older adult at some point in our lives. This trend will continue over the next few

decades due the growing population of those over 65 years of
age. As the number of seniors continues to mount, the need
for care will also. In fact, in the near future families may be
required to care for two or more older relatives at one time.

There is concern that there won't be enough family
members or professionals to fill all the needs. We will be
required to take this situation on as entire extended families
and enlist husbands, siblings, singles, teens, grandchildren,
friends, and so on to fulfill the responsibility of assisting our
elders. Together we must reach out and surround our seniors
with loving care.

Challenges of Giving Care

The growing demand for caregivers puts us in a precarious
position. Much will be asked of us in these roles, in addition to
maintaining a home, job, and our own well-being. We will have
to tap into all of our gifts or acquire those we need including:
knowledge of aging and illnesses, housekeeping skills,
organizational skills, accounting and bookkeeping for medical
bills, patient and compassionate nursing, and love. We also will
fare better if we root ourselves firmly in faith.

Every situation will be unique. How well we are able to give
of ourselves in this way without burning out will depend on the
personalities of the caregiver and receiver, the illnesses
involved, the age of both parties, and their current
abilities/disabilities. It also will be affected by the greatest
variable in the equation, the extent of caregiving required.
Caring for a fairly healthy individual needing a minimal amount
of time and energy or one who has multiple caregivers is
drastically different than caring for someone who is frail,
critically ill, and who requires attention 24 hours a day, seven
days a week from us alone.

People repeatedly tell me their greatest concern about aging
is that they will become a burden on their family. We realize

the strain that caregiving puts on the caregiver, and don't want to subject our loved ones to such a tremendous undertaking. We gladly accept the responsibility to care for our family, but we don't want the tables to be turned. We can't even imagine being the one in need of care.

Older adults who must relinquish control of their basic needs after leading productive, rich lives find the reversal quite humbling. A person who ran a home or business now must submit to someone much younger to care for her very personal and basic needs. We are vulnerable beings. Feelings are easily hurt even when both parties walk the tightrope of caregiving with great caution.

I saw this with my mother. She devoted her life to serving my father and her children. But when she was bedridden with cancer, she had to allow us to care for her. She felt badly that we left our families to assist her. She also did not like that my father took over the housekeeping, laundry, and cooking. Those were responsibilities that defined her purpose for the previous 49 years of their marriage.

Caregiving for a loved one is a very emotional task. Relationship boundaries often shift and blend with the special needs of aging. A daughter bathes a mother. A grandson accompanies his grandfather to doctor visits. The roles and respect due each can get confused.

Caregivers may fall into a mothering role. When extending compassionate care, the parental instinct, naturally, is prompted. But under tremendously stressful conditions, the caregiver must restrain from treating a spouse or elder as a child. The loved one already deals with feelings of inadequacy. They will perceive this treatment as demeaning, even though the caregiver intends no harm.

Caregivers require an endless flow of patience to attend to the countless mishaps, frustrations, and repetitions. Older people with disabilities move slowly. They often want to walk where they are going on their own. Their path will just be taken in little, gradual steps, perhaps with the assistance of a cane or walker. These are times in which we are meant to stroll alongside of them at their pace. They are opportunities to slow down and enjoy the present moment.

A young friend of mine showed me how this works. Frances is an excellent role model for caregiving. She cared for her father who suffered a stroke for more than 15 years. She was patient and joyful as she assisted her dad with all of his needs. Frances truly appeared to be enjoying her father and the opportunity to spend so much time with him. Their reciprocal, fun, and loving relationship was obvious.

Frances' father liked to tell his daughter stories from his past when he worked as a magician. He reminisced about the good old days, and Frances listened as if each time was the first time she heard the story. Some of the episodes took place when Frances was a child, and she remembered them herself. But still, she listened, laughed, and asked her father questions. She encouraged him to talk.

The desire to recant the past is not unusual in older people. This means, however, that caregivers must listen to the same stories again and again. Although this may be boring to us, these are the storyteller's fondest memories. It's best to listen as if we had never heard the story before. To brush it off as something old or unimportant tells the storyteller they are not valued, or that we find them, rather than their tales, tiresome, repetitive, or meaningless.

My father loved to tell stories of his days in the U.S. Navy. He was proud of his service and fellow servicemen. And although his children found them boring, he would repeat the same stories over and over again. Now that he is gone, my brothers, sisters, and I strain to recall the details. We regret that we did not listen better. By not paying attention we not only denied my father validation, we lost a part of our own story.

Listening is a gift we can give to our elders and ourselves. When we pay attention we show how much we value them and the life they led. We also receive the precious gift of their wisdom. In a matter of minutes, we gain a lifetime of lessons. We learn from their diverse experiences.

In addition to a wealth of patience, caregiving also requires physical strength. There is a lot of necessary lifting and pulling. The provider may need to manage a wheel chair, oxygen tank, or other equipment along with attending to the daily personal care of a loved one. If the caregiver also is a senior, their own physical well-being is at a higher risk for a range of illnesses and damage to their own body.

As stated earlier, caregiving also endangers the caregiver's economic security. This is especially so if the total care rests on a sole provider. If our loved one needs care, we must pay an outsider to provide it or care for them ourselves, in which case we may have to take time off from our jobs. Either way, it will cost a lot. We have to trust that we are doing God's work and that God will provide.

We must also deal with other family members. Everyone handles illness and aging differently. If the relative is an emotional or anxious person, they may not cope well and in turn project their frustrations onto us, the caregivers. Perhaps children, step-children, and other close friends and relatives of the care receiver are quick to criticize. They may not appreciate or recognize our daily efforts and level of stress, burdening us further.

And at the end of the day, the care provider may receive little in return for all the hard work we do. The recipient may no longer recognize the provider as friend or family. They also may not be very pleasant or cooperative, resisting every meal, medicinal dosage, and effort to bathe them.

Sometimes the care receiver isn't even someone we particularly feel deserves such a sacrifice. Not all loved ones were good parents, spouses, or partners. They may not have been very loving toward us. They may not be someone who would care for us if we needed them. When this is the case, it is difficult to give so much of ourselves to them.

Even sick, older people of whom we are very fond can be demanding and self-centered. It is not unusual for the recipient to be impatient and expect immediate assistance. Their sense of vulnerability can consume their thoughts. They don't deliberately want to cause stress, but they are prisoners of their condition and cannot think beyond their own needs.

Mostly though, we find it painful to see our loved one age and change. The burly father who protected us from the world; the gentle mother whose arms always were open; or the husband who took on the world for his family seem to be fading away before our eyes. And, if their mental capacity is diminishing, we may no longer have access to their quick wit, problem-solving skills, or sound guidance. We begin to miss "the old them," and find the changes in the relationship to be disheartening.

Dealing with Dementia

Caring for someone with dementia is especially challenging. Dementia is the general term for loss of memory and other mental abilities severe enough to interfere with daily life. Nearly 10 million Americans provided unpaid care for a person with dementia in 2007, according to an Alzheimer Association report. Alzheimer's disease is the most common form of dementia. More than 5 million people in the United States have this disease, which results in one in ten people 65 years of age or older, and nearly half of those over 85.

A caregiver's energy is depleted while caring for someone with dementia more so than with any other illness. With a diagnosis of Alzheimer's we and our loved one embark on a journey to a new dimension where nothing looks, sounds, or feels quite the same. Fantasy and reality intermix in such a way that our conversations may leave us questioning our sanity.

The extent of care and the numerous situations that must be handled every day can wear thin the emotions of even the strongest caregiver. On recent questionnaires, caregivers rated the stress level of caring for a dementia patient as *high* or *very high*. Statistics show that one-third of family caregivers in this situation have symptoms of depression and are more likely to have reduced immune function, hypertension, and coronary heart disease than non-caregivers.

Alzheimer's disease is known as the "long good-bye" because of the way in which the loved one gradually drifts away over an extended period of time. The person becomes increasingly detached emotionally from even people who are closest to them. This prompts a tremendous sense of mourning for family members. It is as if we are desperately trying to hold the hand of someone who is drowning. We hold on tight as they thrash and nearly pull us under, only to have them slip further and further away.

If discovered near the onset, the family may fear a long and challenging road ahead. There is no known cure for Alzheimer's disease, but it is best not to anticipate all the "what ifs." So many variables influence what will happen that no one can predict the exact course the disease will take. And medications are showing tremendous results. Some slow the progression of the disease and help the patient think more clearly for at least a few additional years.

Jesus gave us great advice; "So do not worry about tomorrow, for tomorrow will bring worries of its own. Today's trouble is enough for today" (Matthew 6:34).

Spirituality of Caregiving

Caregivers are presented with a mountain of tasks. It can feel as if we are plunging through an avalanche of responsibilities. Often, people who promise to help are not available nearly enough. As the primary caregiver, our faith can be the lifesaver that gets us through the day.

As I said earlier, I am a caregiver to a loved one with Alzheimer's, and I realize that God's plan for him having this illness has as much to do with me as it does with him. God is placing this situation before me for some reason which I may never know. I trust that since God presented it to me, God will give me what I need to accomplish God's work. I do have times when I feel overwhelmed, but I remind myself—very often—that, "I can do all things through him who strengthens me" (Philippians 4:13).

Every morning I pray that the Holy Spirit blesses my thoughts, words, and actions. I pray, *Veni Sancte Spiritus*—Come Holy Spirit—and ask for the gifts I will need that day. I ask for the light of Christ to shine in, throughout, around, and from me. After that, I trust that I will be given what I need as long as I am doing God's work God's way.

All of us can call on the Holy Spirit and ask for the blessings the Holy Spirit knows we require. There are many "fruits" that are offered to those who live the Word of God including: love, joy, peace, patience, kindness, generosity, faithfulness, gentleness, and self-control (see Galatians 5:22-23). Once we have prayed, we must believe that it is done. We are equipped with all the tools necessary to accomplish the ministry before us.

After learning all of the problems we are facing or will face as caregivers, we still are left with little choice but to accept the challenge. If we have a loved one in our midst who needs our care, we have to see to their well-being. We are to love and serve the Lord by loving and serving one another, beginning with the people in our closest circle.

And we hope that others will do the same for us. No doubt there are countless times in our lives when someone must help us through recovery from an injury or illness. This becomes more likely with age. The longer we live the more we will need medical, nursing, or personal assistance.

While so many women spent their lifetime caring for their family, they may very well be left to fend for themselves in later years. Not only do most senior women live alone, they also comprise three-fourths of nursing home residents 65 and older. When they no longer can care for themselves, they spend their last days in a strange place among strangers. Considering that the typical nursing home resident is a female 85 years of age, and more than half of all women over 65 today will spend at least a day in a nursing home—compared with 33 percent of the male population—many women may very well die outside their own home. And government data shows this is slightly more likely for Caucasians than African Americans.

If we are capable of doing so, we should reach out to our aging loved ones in the same way we hope someone will assist us. There is an opportunity for personal growth in every situation. Caring for seriously ill people can build a foundation for a spiritual friendship. The relationship between caregiver and care-receiver is often intimate and soulful. We may reap incredible spiritual rewards.

This may be especially true when caring for people with dementia because they often have innocence about them. The weight of caring for them is heavy. So much rests entirely on us. But trying to understand their way of thinking forces us to look at everything in our own lives from a different perspective. For example, their need to stay in the present moment will remind us to do the same, instead of worrying about and hurrying to the next activity. If the situation is presented to us, God is sending us a message and a lesson to be learned. Most likely one of those messages is a reminder to appreciate the day the Lord has made.

For older adults who are mentally alert, the end of life can be a time of spiritual awakening and of sharing one's greatest concerns. Through deep reflection, they are likely to become more aware of how God worked in their life. They may come to realize what the important issues really were and how they may have dealt with them differently. The senior also will likely contemplate death and what they may expect in the next life. If we choose to be with them in this time, we will gain from their soul-searching and glimpse what we may experience ourselves, down the line.

Caregiving Coping Strategies

Perhaps the most important thing a caregiver can do for their own well-being is to get plenty of sleep. I often work late into the night. That is when I am most productive because the house is finally quiet. But it is essential that I have sufficient rest and get to bed at a reasonable hour. I never know what the next day will bring. If I'm overtired by mid-morning, I won't be able to handle things with the necessary patience and clear thinking.

Our choice of food and beverage also is important. We must drink plenty of water and maintain a diet that includes fish, especially ones high in omega-3 such as mackerel, lake trout, herring, sardines, albacore tuna, and salmon; vegetables, especially leafy greens, Brussels sprouts, broccoli, beets, avocados, and red bell peppers, and berries. We also may wish to supplement our diet with good multivitamins, calcium with vitamin D, and minerals.

Caregivers also should caution against setting unrealistic expectations. Attention surrounds an older, infirmed family member, and rightly so. Doctors, counselors, and other medical providers instruct caregivers with their extensive recommendations of care. But the lengthy list given is often impossible for one person to provide. No matter how hard we work, we cannot complete everything. Feelings of inadequacy are sure to result.

Finding strategies to meet the needs of our loved one without neglecting those of other family members (and ourselves) is vital. Remember that we do not have to do everything ourselves. Our responsibility is to see that our loved one is cared for, but not at the expense of our own health.

That only puts the responsibility of our care in the hands of someone else.

The NFCA (National Family Caregivers Association) suggests that caregivers make a list of tasks that need to be done and then categorize the items in their order of importance. We should look closely to see which items can be omitted or given to someone else. Call on our spouse, children, and siblings to participate in our family member's care. Friends and other people in the community may assist us as well.

In a church community, there are many ways those who are not caring for someone can relieve stress from a parishioner who is. One of my fellow parishioners belonged to our parish's Prayer Shawl Ministry and made a beautiful soft, pink shawl for me. She prayed for me each time she picked up her knitting needles, and one of our priests blessed the shawl when it was completed. I received the shawl in a gift bag with a note and a prayer that, even still, brings me to tears. I am so touched by the time and love my sister in Christ worked into every stitch. Each time I see it, I am reminded that I am wrapped in love, prayer, and support.

We also can give the caregiver a break from their 24/7 responsibilities by donating a few hours a week to caring for their loved one. Chances are, even if the care receiver is a bit cranky, she will be quite appreciative and more considerate with us, an outsider, than family. Or we can run errands, mow the lawn, shovel snow, prepare a meal, sort through medical bills and insurance papers, clean house, or make minor home repairs or improvements.

If we are a senior ourselves and are in good health, we can offer our companionship. Homebound people look forward to short visits, especially from peers. We can reminisce about the good old days or enjoy a game of cards. Sometimes it is enjoyable simply to sit together watching television from an EZ chair or relish the trees rustling in the breeze from the front-porch bench. What the homebound wants most is our presence.

Extending Tender Loving Care

In a just society, those who are able care for those who need
assistance. It is our responsibility to look after one another.
With so many people approaching their senior years, we will
have to open our arms wider than ever. We will definitely have
our hands full, nurturing and caring for loved ones in need.

Sometimes it is the caregiver who needs us most. Be a
friend to either the caregiver or receiver and we help them
both. Perhaps this gift will be extended to us someday. After
all, if we are not in one of those positions at present, we may
well be soon. It is very likely that we too will have to count on
someone to care for us, at least for short periods of time
before we die.

We are told repeatedly in Scripture to love one another. It
is easy to love someone who is young, beautiful, and fun. It is
quite another to reach out to the feeble and infirmed or one in
the midst of agony. But this is our Christian obligation. We
are to love one another, to be God to one another, for God
is love.

The rewards for such work are astronomical. When we do
love one another, God is in us and we are in God. We become
infused with the Spirit. Scripture says, "By this we know that
we abide in him and he in us, because he has given us of his
Spirit" (1 John 4:13). What an incredible gift for our efforts.

*Lord, you are my rock and my salvation.
I trust the Holy Spirit to supply me with all I need to
care for the seniors in my life.*

Strengthening Spirituality Through Suffering and Loss

Endless rounds of golf, hobby clubs, exotic travel, and visiting with grandchildren: this is the retirement dream. After a long life of labor in and outside of the home, fun and restful days await us. The closer we get to the magic age of 65, focus intensifies on that dream. Our many decades of hard work are about to pay off.

Unfortunately, the reality is that only some (and sometimes none) of the fantasy retirement comes true. The later years are mixed with various proportions of joy and heartache. Some seniors have few issues and enjoy the vision in its entirety. But the majority experience hills and valleys of grief and happiness, good health and illness. There also are seniors who suffer greatly throughout their advanced years or die before retirement ever really begins. They never cash in on one minute of their dream.

Jeanie, a friend of mine, and I were discussing the extensive number of friends we know who are seriously ill. Jeanie commented that the senior years are supposed to be golden, but to her they really seemed to be only dirt. She was joking to some extent, but she also was frustrated and saddened by the struggles good people were going through. She did not understand why so many had to suffer.

We all know someone who was close to retirement and died suddenly from a stroke or heart attack. The experience can leave survivors feeling that they too were somehow cheated. It hardly seems fair that the friend's life should end in such a way, or that we should be deprived of their companionship when we so desperately need them. Illness, losing our friends, and our own impending death certainly tests our spiritual strength.

Yet, faithful people know on some level that all of this is a part of God's plan. Even our suffering is a God-given gift. God always is kind, merciful, and just, so all the difficulties must be for our own good—or that of the world's.

A simple yet profound responsorial often repeated in churches declares this belief.

> Presider: God is good.
> Parishioners: All the time.
> Presider: All the time.
> Parishioners: God is good.

Perhaps the best lesson is to remember that God is with us through it all, the tough and the easy times. Pope emeritus, His Holiness, Benedict XVI, said that when we are suffering, we should trust God. "Don't doubt God's presence," he told a gathering at the Cardinal Paul-Emile Leger Centre in Yaounde, Cameroon, on March 19, 2009. "You are not alone in your pain, for Christ himself is close to all who suffer."

Letting Go

Loss is an inevitable component of aging. The longer we live, and greater we are blessed, the more we have to lose. Slowly we will detach voluntarily or forcefully from people and things that were once very meaningful to us. One by one we will say good-bye to countless friends and relatives. We will have to let go of our work, home, and furnishings. What we do not release by our own volition will be taken away from us in preparation

for our departure from this world and our entrance into
the next.

But this loss also is a blessing. An older couple who attends
the same church that I do lost their home and all of their
belongings in Hurricane Katrina in 2005. They relocated to my
parish on the invitation of family members who helped them
regroup. Surprisingly, the couple said that they soon found the
forced removal of all the stuff of their life to be freeing and
refreshing. They hadn't previously realized how the weight of
their clutter consumed energies they now spend enjoying one
another and their family.

With time, pieces of our earthly self vanish naturally little
by little. Hair thins, vision weakens, and hearing diminishes.
We can't move or think as quickly as we once did. Pulling
ourselves out of bed or getting up from a chair takes some
maneuvering. Words and names are difficult to retrieve, and
thoughts rise only to vanish before we can verbalize them. Of
course there also are those gains that come with age—wrinkles,
false teeth, knee and hip replacements, and a mid-section of
unwanted pounds.

Humor aside, we do have to marvel at the gift of life. The
human body is a masterpiece. We are capable of incredible
mental and physical achievements. With today's technologies,
we also can overcome an array of devastating illnesses and
disabilities. However, although the body works and heals
itself with prayer and medical assistance in amazing ways, it is
not invincible. Our mortal bodies are subject to breakdowns
and disease. We can't expect them to run year after year
without periodic maintenance and repairs. Eventually, our
bodies will expire.

The harder we are on our bodies and the longer we are
allowed to use them, the more likely it is that damage will
occur. Some of this is by our own abuse and neglect. Cigarette
smoking, overeating artery-clogging foods, lack of exercise,
alcohol and drug abuse, and an abundance of stress harm the
body and mind in countless ways. These factors contribute

toward high blood pressure, high cholesterol, diabetes, obesity, and other diseases by our own choices. Paying attention to the early warning signs of mental and physical illness and disease and seeking proper medical attention as promptly as possible also is important.

And then there are the people who seem to do everything right. They are good, hardworking people who care for their health. They put great thought into what they eat and do but still get sick. A common remark when illness strikes people like that is, "Why me? What did I do to deserve such misfortune?" It is as if there must be a direct correlation between what we do and what happens to us, or that we are too good for suffering, which simply isn't so.

Purpose to Pain

Ancient cultures thought that illness was a divine punishment. The sick person or their ancestors failed God in some way and got what they deserved. Associating with someone who was diseased or who worked in an unethical job harmed other people's health as well. They believed that if they went near someone who was sick or disabled, then they would receive the same fate. Sickness was considered a curse and the curse was thought to be contagious.

Jesus declared this theory was wrong. He ministered to the sick and maimed—even people with leprosy, a greatly feared condition. He reached out to outcasts with kindness. When asked if a blind man or his parents had sinned and caused the man's disability, Jesus answered, "Neither this man nor his parents sinned" (John 9:3). Jesus continued to say that the sufferer was God's instrument. The man became blind so "that God's work might be revealed in him."

In difficult situations, we sway toward increased or decreased faith. But illness might be a particularly influential tool for faith development. The *Catechism of the Catholic Church* states that, "illness and suffering have always been among the gravest problems confronted in human life. In illness, man experiences his powerlessness, his limitations, and his fortitude. Every illness can make us glimpse death" (1500). The *Catechism* goes on to say that illness can lead to despair and revolt against God. However, "it can also make a person more mature, helping him discern in his life what is not essential so that he can turn toward that which is. Very often illness provokes a search for God and a return to him" (1501).

We can't possibly know the reasons for agony and loss. We can only trust that God knows and works in our best interest. The people and things of this world fade beyond our grasp: our focus intensifies on the Lord. God alone demands our attention.

Everything is a part of God's plan for the greater good. We believe this is true because we believe in a merciful and gracious God. When we are willing to experience and accept pain and suffering, acceptance transforms into something else. We allow God's work to be revealed through us like the blind man in Scripture.

Our struggle or loss may be a catalyst for something greater. It may prompt us to search for meaning in our lives: our soul purpose—rather than sole purpose—for living. Ironically, people often say that they appreciate their life so much more since being diagnosed with a life-threatening illness. The sickness served as a wake-up call that the end of their life may be near. Any changes or amends they wanted to make were best done right away.

Some people who deliberately put themselves in harm's way understand this. Bullfighter Cayetano Rivera Ordonez talked about the dangers of bullfighting in an interview on *60 Minutes* (April 19, 2009). Being so close to death, in the ring, makes him feel more alive. Hopefully, most of us don't have to intentionally step into danger to appreciate the present moment.

Often at the end of life, people remark on what they would have done differently had they the opportunity to live it over. Common sentiments include wishing they traveled more and spent less time worrying or fussing over minor irritations or things for which they had no control. Most often, they regret not spending more time with loved ones or less time with angry, foul people. We can learn from them and periodically stop and think about this even if we are not currently experiencing danger, pain, or loss.

Another reason for suffering is that it allows Christ's light to shine. Caregiving and receiving care offers an incredible opportunity for both parties to grow tremendously in faith. No one wants to be dependent on another individual for their basic daily needs, but when we must, we move toward dependency on Christ. We are forced to trust ourselves into the hands of those who not only give of themselves but also the Christ within them. The caregiver is Christ to those who receive care. Spiritually, this is a win/win situation for both parties.

Mainly, suffering prompts us to get down on our knees. It provides groundwork for building faith. Our pain draws us closer to God and encourages a better line of communication through prayer. Scripture says, "Give all your worries and cares to God, for he cares about what happens to you" (1 Peter 5:7).

Relinquishing our troubles to God is a good method of coping. Older people who are religious and turn toward their faith in times of trouble show lower levels of mortality, depression, suicide, anxiety, and alcohol abuse according to several studies. They know that worry has no value. The outcome of our struggles is not in our control, and so we are left with nothing to fuss over.

However, the *Catechism of the Catholic Church* reminds us that "even the most intense prayers do not always obtain the healing of all illnesses. Thus St. Paul must learn from the Lord that 'my grace is sufficient for you, for my power is made perfect in weakness' and that the sufferings to be endured can mean that in my flesh I complete what is lacking in Christ's afflictions for the sake of his Body, that is, the Church" (1508).

Our pain also can serve as an opportunity to share in Christ's Passion. It is believed that, in a limited way, when we offer our pain to God we take on some of what Christ bore for our sins. EWTN news anchor, Raymond Arroyo tells a remarkable story of the network's founder, Mother Angelica (Mother Mary Angelica/Rita Antoinette Rizzo). Arroyo says that Mother Angelica has lived with pain most of her life. But she also told him that when the pain is the most severe, she knows God is the closest.

Once when Mother Angelica was gasping for breath in the midst of a severe asthma attack, she begged Jesus to hold her. She then felt Jesus' love surround her, and slowly she began to breathe. Before her was a vision of Jesus on the cross. She witnessed his agony first hand. Mother Angelica believed that the incident was not only an opportunity for healing, but it also allowed her to experience some of Jesus' pain (Arroyo, 251).

The reasons for suffering offered here are not intended to glorify suffering. Nor are they intended to minimize our levels of grief. If we are experiencing loss, suffering, or sorrow, the experience is painful no matter why we have to endure it. When illness and tragedy strike, it is difficult to keep the faith. It is not uncommon to feel that God does not hear our prayers. That God has abandoned us. But God promised us that would never happen (Deuteronomy 4:31).

Only God knows why we have to suffer. But God does hear us and answers us in ways that are God's alone. With prayer and trust in God, relief will come. We have Jesus' promise for peace in the next life, if not in this one. That is his gift to us.

Serving Those Who Suffer

We can be of great assistance to the sick and needy by praying
for them. Pain is very distracting. Chronic health conditions
and diseases make it difficult to concentrate on prayer.
Focusing on Jesus or Mary and submitting our pain to them
may not be possible in the midst of our agony. These are
occasions when people in pain are most grateful to friends who
remember them in their prayers. Scripture says, "The prayer of
faith will save the sick" (James 5:15).

We also may encourage those who suffer to receive the
sacraments as often as possible. Great healing is found in the
Eucharist, Reconciliation, and the Anointing of the Sick.
Sacraments are signs instituted by Christ that give grace. And it
is God's grace on which we are carried through stressful and
trying times.

The sacrament of the Anointing of the Sick was formerly
known as Extreme Unction and administered only one time at
the point of death. It included confession, anointing, and
viaticum—the Eucharist as food for the passage through death
to Eternal Life. Today the sacraments of Reconciliation,
Anointing, and the Eucharist are administered separately. Also,
we are allowed to receive the Anointing of the Sick as needed
and more often for the purpose of healing.

Every life is to be valued in its entirety, from beginning to
end. This holds those who are in good health in a spiritually
critical place. How we treat our most vulnerable brothers and
sisters is indicative of who we are. It is the grounds on which
we will be judged. As stated earlier, providing adequate
housing, food, and medical care to the needy of all ages is the
basic responsibility of those who are advantaged.

In addition, we can reach out to those who feel alone,
unnecessary, and unwanted. Elderly people often suffer from
"chronic problem personality," that is they may be angry,
depressed, anxious, and/or delusional. Most likely they are
unaware of the impact these conditions have on others. It

certainly is not their intention to stress out the people who are entrusted with their care. Although it is not easy, we have to keep in mind that they are suffering.

Another option for helping people in need is to make ourselves available to those who live alone. Aging, especially when advanced, often parallels loneliness. Ironically, we can feel quite alone in this crowded, hectic, and noisy world. Older men are more likely to be married, but nearly half of women aged 75 or more live alone. Many women never were married or no longer are. They may have children but prefer to live independently, finding the activity in a busy household with young grandchildren to be too stressful. And as stated earlier, only five percent live in nursing homes at the very end of their lives, even though a number of them have serious mental or physical health issues. The resulting isolation of independent living is known to promote illness and premature death.

Interestingly, Japan is experiencing a situation unlike anything before in their history due to so many of their seniors living alone. The country is seeing an alarming rise in petty crime by their 65 and over population. This group has doubled in size yet has committed five times the number of crimes in the last two decades. This is thought to stem from seniors' sense of abandonment. The Japanese culture traditionally held elders in high regard, caring for them tenderly. That scenario is much rarer today. The result is behavior similarly found in children who misbehave. It is believed that some older people seek attention and a connection with others through their negative behavior.

Sometimes we serve our seniors simply by listening. Young people find it amusing how older people give a lengthy response, rather than the pat answer of "fine," when asked how they are. As we move into that realm, we suddenly understand. Health issues consume much of our daily thoughts and concerns, but no one really wants to hear about them. Extending an open ear to someone who is not well is a precious gift.

Providing some humor is good for everyone's health as well. Usually it is the silly little everyday things in life that are humorous. Do we know a story or joke they may find funny? Do we have time to sit and watch a comedy with them? An opportunity for fun can be just the right medicine.

One Christmas I had the pleasure of reading a children's version of the nativity story to a delightful child named Alexis, who was three-years-old at the time. While we read, we found the different characters in my wooden nativity set. Alexis listened intently as she lined up the shepherds, kings, and lambs. At the end of the story she asked me to read it again, only this time with the funny parts.

"Funny parts?" I asked.

"Yes," she insisted. "You skipped the funny parts."

"This isn't a funny story, Alexis. I don't think there are any funny parts."

"There always are funny parts," she said. "Want me to tell you the story with the funny parts?"

And she proceeded to tell her own version of the nativity story with quite an interesting twist of humor.

I've laughed a lot thinking about Alexis' unusual take on Jesus' birth. I've also come to realize that this precious child most likely was correct. When we trust in the Lord and live joyfully, we are happy and can look at even the most challenging situations with some levity.

Joseph and Mary certainly did trust in God and the path God laid for them. Maybe as they struggled to find shelter and ended up giving birth in a stable, Joseph teased Mary about the story they would tell their newborn son one day in regards to his unusual birth. And animals can be playful and humorous to watch. They must have taken great interest in Jesus' birth. Maybe Mary and Joseph laughed at the animals' reactions to what was unfolding.

Even in the midst of our saddest moments, we often find humor in the oddest things. Bringing those stories to our seniors allows them the opportunity to laugh along with us.

When we enter their presence joyfully, we may be quite surprised at their response.

From This Life to the Next

The very old often remark how surprised they are that they have lived so long. But God makes no mistakes. There is a purpose for every moment of our existence, and perhaps the last years or months are the greatest. The reason for that person's longevity also may not have as much to do with them as the people around them. Perhaps they remain here to teach the following generations how to age with dignity and purpose and die with grace.

There is a theory that all of our fears boil down to a fear of death. Snakes, crowds, water, and heights are triggers for the fear that death will result. Aging can be added to that list. We avoid aging not because we don't want to live as an older person as much as we don't want to be reminded that with aging, death is sure to follow.

Our anxiety is partly because we rarely see death actually happen. Few of us have witnessed someone taking their last breath. This lack of experience makes us feel unqualified and incapable of sending off our loved ones to the next life. When death appears to be approaching we quickly shuffle them off to hospitals and nursing homes so they may die in the hands of professionals and out of sight of the living. The result is that we perpetuate the lack of experience and fear death more. We continue to deny the reality that we all will die.

Personally, I feel blessed to have spent so much time with both of my parents before they died. We had many heartfelt discussions about what they thought about their lives as well as their impending death. I asked my mother if she regretted not traveling more or not using her college education in the work force after having her children. She said she had no regrets. She felt privileged to devote her time to her family and very thankful for the gift of faith her parents helped her develop.

Neither of my parents was afraid to die. In fact they were quite calm and peaceful in the knowledge that they were going home. My father was especially ready. My mother passed away three years before him, and he missed her terribly. He was excited to see her again. For Dad, death was not a sentence but rather a reward.

My parents taught me how to die a good death. When they received their diagnosis of advanced cancers, they let go of their material things, said their farewells, and spiritually prepared for their ultimate journey as best they knew how. They prayed, confessed, and gave thanks. They departed content and ready.

We have public, contemporary leaders who taught us how to end this life peacefully as well. These role models showed us how to live as spiritual beings in each and every moment. Mother Teresa of Calcutta and Cardinal Joseph Bernadin are prime examples.

Blessed Pope John Paul II also taught us much about life and death. He was a powerful catechist and evangelizer even in an old and feeble state. When advanced Parkinson Disease caused difficulty with his speech and movements, when he no longer looked the part of a powerful leader, he refused to hide from public view. Rather he showed us his spiritual strength in his bodily weakness.

Anyone who witnessed the televised clips of Blessed John Paul's final days knows this to be true. He was the father of the Catholic Church, our Papa Wojtlyla, until his final breath. Upon his death, more than 600,000 people proved this by waiting in line to pray before his body in the Vatican basilica. The world was greatly blessed by this incredible man and his example of how to live and die in faith.

Our lives are like the infinitely different snowflakes that fall gently and then quickly vanish leaving only a wet kiss to mark their brief existence. Death is inevitable. "For everything there is a season, and a time for every matter under heaven: A time to be born, and a time to die; a time to plant, and a time to pluck up what is planted" (Ecclesiastes 3:1-2). Eventually all of us will die. Our bodies will disintegrate and turn to dust. It is a part of the normal rhythm of life.

The Pascal Mystery tells us that we have to die to rise again. We have to let go to be fully free. A person attains spiritual maturity when he or she comes to realize that existence is not in one's own hands. We exist in this world only as long as God breathes life into us. "When you hide your face, they are/ dismayed;/ when you take away their breath,/ they die" (Psalm 104:29).

Christians benefit greatly from the knowledge that with death comes a new life of peace, joy, and reunion with loved ones already passed. We also believe in the resurrection of our bodies at the end of time. When we die our soul will go to God. At the end of the world as we know it, our body will rise from the dead and reunite with the soul. We then will go body and soul to heaven.

The Christian funeral rite of Burial reminds us that we are one with all the baptized, living and dead, and one with the communion of saints. As indicated by the Second Council of Nicea, Council of Florence, Council of Trent, and stated in The Apostles' Creed, we are in spiritual union with the saints in heaven, souls in purgatory, and all the living faithful. Whatever our age, we continue to be an integral part of the whole. We remain in unity with all who have died through a continuous set of meaningful, symbolic rites and practices. The one who died simultaneously remains alive with us and also now is united with the angels and loved ones who previously passed.

Catholics begin and end our physical life in the church through the sacraments as evidenced by the rituals that parallel infant baptism and the funeral Mass. Both begin at the door of the church with the congregation gathered at baptism with the child, marking the beginning of a pilgrimage in faith, and at the funeral with the casket, marking the presentation back to God.

Whereas the baby is baptized with Holy Water, the coffin is sprinkled with Holy Water in remembrance of the baptismal waters. The white garment worn at baptism is symbolized by the use of a large white cloth, called a pall, which is placed over the coffin. Also the candles that are lit and given to the godparents at baptism are remembered at the funeral service with the paschal candle, both of which symbolize the light of Christ.

Gift of the Present

My husband, son, and I once took a cabin cruiser out on the Atlantic Ocean. We were enjoying the sun and the water when we suddenly found ourselves surrounded by sharks. As they continued to circle closer around our boat, our concerns mounted. Then we realized that they were not sharks but dolphins—playful, happy dolphins. The frightening experience transformed into an enjoyable one.

Our perception of a situation influences our reaction and behavior. The animals surrounding us did not change on that day on the Atlantic—nor did their behavior—but, ours did. We no longer felt threatened, but rather blessed.

The same is true for suffering, loss, caregiving, and other challenges of aging. When we view a situation as an opportunity to serve, love, or submit and trust in the Lord, it is no longer overwhelming. It becomes an experience of joy. We find ourselves more gentle and giving with the people in our lives, growing in faith, and moving closer to God.

This world is not heaven. It is greatly flawed because of humanity's many sins. The result is the aging, suffering, and dying that is a part of the cycle of life. We cannot avoid agony and death. Many saints suffered. Christ suffered. Why wouldn't we expect to do the same?

Eight out of ten Americans age 65 or older are living with some form of chronic illness according to a report by the U.S.

Centers for Disease Control and Prevention (2007). Regardless of the pain, a survey conducted on behalf of the National Women's Health Resource Center found that women have a positive outlook on aging. Life is a gift and a joy despite its struggles if we perceive the challenges as adventures and opportunities.

One of the greatest concerns for many of the most faithful Christians is that they die in a state of grace. This was a response written repeatedly on the questionnaire I sent out to middle-and senior-aged adults. Although they believed they were saved through Christ's passion, responders worried that they did not do enough good or avoid enough evil. Most of these people are actively involved in the church and continuously strive to grow in their faith, so I found their responses surprising. It seems ironic to me that the people who seemingly work the hardest to follow their faith are the most concerned about their success in doing so.

When determined to live a holy life worthy of God's approval, we can keep in mind the Alcoholic Anonymous saying, "Just do the next right thing." We don't have to do everything there is to do all at once—simply concentrate on the most pressing item on the list. Once that is completed, we can move on to the next one. If we follow this pattern, before we know it we will have accomplished a life-long string of "right things."

Religious Sister of Providence Mary Roger Madden said that she believes in the sacrament of the present moment. "I live not one day but one minute at a time, striving to accept whatever is required of me in that minute," she said. "When death comes, it will be just one more of those minutes. Before Jesus left the earth, he promised to come back and take us to the place he has prepared for us. I hope to be conscious to welcome him when he comes."

I know, Lord, you are with me every moment of every day. Through every joy and tribulation, I trust in you, Lord Jesus.

Strengthening Spirituality by Sharing Our Story

How would we have learned of creation or salvation without the passing of stories from one person to another, generation after generation, throughout history? Would we know about Adam and Eve, Moses, or Jesus if ancient people had not told their children about them?

We are a people of God called to spread the Word. Our ancestors were so moved that they repeated their spiritual experiences. They passed the torch of faith to their children, friends, and neighbors who in turn passed it on. We must do this as well.

God and humanity are not two different stories. We are God's creation. Everything about us and around us is because of and about God. This makes our story God's story. Acknowledging the goodness and mercy of our Lord in our lives, and how God connects us to one another, is an important part in telling the whole story of humanity.

Intergenerational Relationships

When we extend our hand in friendship, we share our spiritual story. Friendships are a gift from God and vital to our sense of well-being. They offer a means to share our selves, God's creations, with others also created by God. In a sense, friendships allow us to continue beyond our own life by touching and remaining with another human being long after we are gone from this world.

We are social creatures and thrive when interconnected with others. Studies on longevity show this to be true. It is the people in our lives who inspire us to be better, stronger, and happier. They keep us going through the tough times, reminding us to just put one foot in front of the other. We gain and give strength and a sense of being loved and valued in these healthy relationships.

The *Catechism of the Catholic Church* states, "the principle of solidarity, also articulated in terms of 'friendship' or 'social charity,' is a direct demand of human and Christian brotherhood" (1939). In a sense then, friendship is an obligation. We are commanded to connect with one another.

At one time, intergenerational households, or even extended visits with family members of other generations, were very common. Few families have several generations in the same home anymore. Currently, women are having children at an older age, resulting in significantly older grandparents, most of whom live a distance away. This development minimizes the opportunity for interaction between generations, which is unfortunate.

Being friends with people the same age—or older— becomes more difficult for older people who watch friend after friend pass away. Even when they move into senior housing, retirement centers, and nursing homes where they are exposed to other people their age to befriend, many feel any effort to do so will be futile. One can only bear so much loss. It makes little sense to become friends with more people only to watch them fade out of our life too.

A viable solution for maintaining friendships throughout our life is to develop friendships with people of all ages. Intergenerational relationships offer so many opportunities for personal growth and happiness. The enthusiasm and energy of the young complement the wisdom and patience of the old. This makes friendships within and between the generations essential.

It is a blessing to have several friends who are a number of years older than us, especially if they are generous with their knowledge, guidance, and support. We can go to them with questions or concerns and tap into their insight. Through them we can come to understand things in different ways than we could have without them.

Peers close in age are fun to be with because we share the culture of the same generation. We enjoy the same music, activities, and history. We "remember when" together. Our physical experiences as we age also offer a common point of understanding. We sympathize and commiserate together over the struggles of aging.

If possible, we also should have a number of friends who are younger than we are, some of whom might be significantly younger. These friends will be wise in ways we are not. Their world is so different than ours was when we were their age. They can encourage us to see things differently than our tried and true predictable way and keep us thinking with a more open mind.

Younger friends help us to remain in the present and less in the past. These relationships encourage us to be more open to new ideas and less stuck in the rut of having things the same way day after day. In addition the span of ages provides a wider range of skills and activities to consider.

Younger people haven't encountered a lifetime of obstacles and setbacks and therefore are more hopeful and dreamy. They remind seniors of the possibilities. Their hunger for excitement and fun can be contagious, prompting us to remain young and vibrant along with them.

On the other hand, younger people gain from the experience of seniors. Rather than figuring everything out for themselves, they can tap into the wealth of a lifetime seniors

offer them. They have a window to the past and events that led
to the world in which they currently live. Scripture advises,
"Remember the days of old,/ consider the years long past;/ ask
your father, and he will inform/ you; your elders, and they will
tell you" (Deuteronomy 32:7). We don't have to figure
everything out ourselves. Instead, we can learn from the older
people who already have lived similar experiences.

Younger people who are exposed to elders also can observe
the aging process. The younger and middle aged persons may
fear the visible signs of aging. Most likely, they then also fear
death. Friendships across generations alleviate some of the
fear. They show that every age has its beauty and advantages.

Investing in the Future

One of the greatest gifts seniors can give the young is to
mentor them. Mentoring encompasses a vast range of ways
that help protégés blossom and grow. It is the sharing of a
life-time of knowledge, experience, talent, and wisdom
that helps open doors. It is an investment of oneself into
future generations.

Mentoring can happen in any area of our lives. Whatever
way we would like to grow or share is a potential area on which
to build a mentoring relationship. The older we get the more
we know. This cultivates an endless assortment of talents and
skills which we can contribute. Marriage, child rearing,
friendships, co-workers, faith, technology, finances, medicine,
sewing, cooking, home repairs and decorating are some
examples. Sharing our experiences eliminates the need for our
protégé to learn everything about that topic from the bottom
up. Together we may enjoy a rich pool of wisdom, ideas, and
creativity. And when we are spiritual, our beliefs and values are
incorporated into our perspective on what we mentor.

Some of my fondest childhood memories are of cooking
with my Grandma Rose and Aunty Antoinette. When I was a

child, my grandmother often stayed with our family for months at a time. Not only did I learn from my grandmother and her sister, my great aunt, how to prepare Italian dishes from scratch, I learned about life. By listening to their stories while they cooked, they made it easy for me to talk to them about my own concerns. Regardless of the years between us, our deepest worries, happiness, and desires were not very different. Through the sharing of their experiences, I learned how I might resolve my own.

Look around where you live, work, and pray. Opportunities to mentor, as well as be mentored, are everywhere. Perhaps we aren't very familiar with the other person with whom we wish to build this relationship. Successful mentoring is not even dependent on the congeniality of the mentor and protégé. The two people involved do not have to be great friends. A respect for the shared gifts and the individuals sharing them is all that is required. In fact, people of differing cultures, faiths, and backgrounds challenge us to not only understand others more clearly but also understand our selves better.

Nor does the mentoring relationship have to be a part of any formal program. We can simply talk to each other, or if possible, demonstrate how we do something so that the inexperienced can learn firsthand. We also can mentor remotely via telephone, text, Skype, or email. Younger generations are very comfortable with these forms of communication.

I have a deeper relationship with nieces, nephews, and the older step-grandchildren because I meet them where they are most comfortable—through texting and social media. I also have "spoken" with one of my favorite mentors, Sister Alexa, through e-mail. Sister Alexa is in her 90s yet can quickly respond and support me in a way that is convenient for me. That is what a good mentor does.

Spiritual Autobiography

Genealogy, the discovery and documentation of ancestry, is a popular hobby today because people are realizing that the past continues to be a part of who we are. Each and every person in our family tree has a place of honor and relates in some way to the whole. Like it or not, we are affected by the people in our life, and we have an impact on them. We are not individuals created by chance to act independently. Rather we are a chain of humanity linked one by one from the first people God created until the very last. Acknowledging each and every link gives value to the work of God in all of us.

Our seniors are our link to the past. They are the historians who pass on the stories of relatives we never met and ones we hardly knew. Preserving the stories through audio, video, or written documentation is an important key to our own identity. Should we want to know more from one of our relatives, there is no time to waste.

Recreating a portrait of their personal voyage through life may serve as a means for healing on several levels. Therapists often assist seniors, especially those who are ill or advanced in age, with remembering the details of their past. By constructing such a memoir, the senior realizes the significance of their life. Humans have a need to tell their unique story. Recounting the glory days can be quite enjoyable. Doing so helps put the tidbits of our lives into perspective and makes us feel valued and understand what we did and why.

Biographies are a favorite genre. There is much to learn about ourselves by reading how other people took their potpourri of experiences, those they chose and those they had thrust upon them, and assembled them into their life. Through them we recognize our own strengths, weaknesses, achievements, failings, and potential. We are reminded that God created us to be special and unique and that every one of us has something to offer, something to teach, to share.

Retrieving special moments nestled deeply in the past also is a way to stimulate brain activity for older people struggling to hang on to the details of their life. It is a mental geriatric workout that therapists use toward better mental health. Through this therapy, some parts of the brain left dormant for decades are activated once again.

We can try this ourselves. We can collect the memories of our pasts in tangible ways through scrapbooking, writing a memoir, compiling a photo album, or audio or video recording. This process reveals a self-definition, the way in which we perceive ourselves. How much we want to include about our profession; the people, places, and things we loved; and how we want to be remembered reveal our values.

The compilation also serves as a useful historical tool. Our autobiography presents documentation for our family and local organizations. It can assist with family genealogy and help illustrate ancestries for the generations that follow. The story of our lives connects the past with the present and the present with the future.

However, remembering does come with some risk. Sadness may result from the realization that the end of this life is approaching. What was loved and cherished most is slipping through our hands. The activity may promote self-pity, depression, fear, or even anger. Unresolved disappointments, injustices committed or received, and feelings of inadequacy may surface.

Although such emotions are uncomfortable, the exercise can function as an opportunity to confront the issues before it is too late. Once we acknowledge a past hurt, we can offer or ask for forgiveness and make amends. Releasing this pain is tremendously healing for the body and soul.

In addition to creating a book of adventures and achievements, we may consider preparing a spiritual autobiography. Through such memoirs, we will learn how to build on our own relationship with the Lord. We can teach them about God by telling of God's presence and work in our lives. We show the many ways in which we are blessed.

This collection is an important part of our legacy of faith. It can be written on the computer or in our own handwriting. Once completed, we may print and bind it as a traditional book at our local office supply store or simply insert it into a spiral notebook.

The scrapbook method for preserving and illustrating our spirituality is another option. In addition to our personal, living example as a Christian, spiritual scrapbooking, or faithbooking, as it often is called, is an avenue to evangelize and share our faith. We can include certificates and photos for baptism, confirmation and marriage; journal entries; Scripture versus; clippings from newspapers, magazines, or Sunday church bulletins; holy cards; and remembrances from wake and funeral services. We can add stories of situations when God moved us in directions we would not otherwise have taken or rescued us from physically or spiritually dangerous situations.

Faithbooking is more than documenting our marriage, children or jobs. Rather, it shows how God influenced us as a faithful person. Our faithbook may be all-encompassing, exploring the many ways God has touched us. We also may touch on when God felt far away. Sharing examples of the times we struggled with our faith is as important as when we did not. Our loved ones can learn greatly from our examples.

Our faithbook may be a project we work on for many years. We can be as creative and detailed as we wish. We will find that the extensive display of thoughts and experiences results in an inspiring example of faith for our own reflection as well as our family and friends.

God Remembers

Memory is essential to our well-being, but why do we forget so much as we grow older? For some, it is a challenge to recall all but the most significant events and details. And even the events that once defined us fade away. In later stages of Alzheimer's, many do not even know their own name. They live purely in the moment. The past is left behind bit by bit, and the future is of no concern whatsoever.

Perhaps this is all part of the spiritual lesson we learn from God's name. God said his name is "I Am." God did not call himself, "I Was" or "I Will Be." God's name is of the present, the now. This is a curious point to ponder. If God's concerns are with the present moment *only*, we simply need to concern ourselves with our current thoughts and actions. Fretting over what did happen, or what may happen, should not be on our radar. The time to think and act is now.

It also is interesting to note how the Holy Spirit inspired the writers of Scripture. God's great love and mercy is evident in the history of humanity's relationship with God, but Scripture does not list the blessings God gave us. Nor does it ask for a detailed account of our activities and accomplishments. Basically, we only need to know that God remembers us and we remember God.

This is crucial: to be remembered by God is to be held in existence, to live. If God forgot us we would be dead, not as in the opposite of alive but in the way of nonexistence. Psalm 88 says that a person whom God's wrath lies heavy upon is one whom God has forgotten.

But we do not have to worry about God forgetting us. God promised that will never happen. And God's promise extends to us even if we forget God. Scripture says, "Can a woman forget her nursing child, or show no compassion for the child of her womb? Even these you may forget, yet I will not forget you" (Isaiah 49:15). God illustrates this promise throughout history. When Israel violated the covenant with God with her immoral and unfaithful ways, God continued to remember Israel. (See Ezekiel 16:59-60.)

God remembers the faithful by responding to our prayers. God answered Samson's request to remember and strengthen

him (Judges 16:28). God remembered Rachel and Hannah by
answering their prayers for a child. (See Genesis 30:22 and 1
Samuel 1:11, 19-20.) God also remembered the covenant with
Noah that water will never destroy all humanity with a flood
(Genesis 9:15) and the covenant with Abraham, Isaac, and
Jacob (Exodus 2:24 and Leviticus 26:42, Deuteronomy 9:27).

God remembers not only those individuals but all the
people of Israel and their covenant with God as well as all
people of all times. "When the bow is in the clouds, I will
see it and remember the everlasting covenant between God
and every living creature of all flesh that is on the earth"
(Genesis 9:16).

As God remembers us, God forgives and forgets our
offenses. For example, God promised Israel that their sins
were no longer remembered. (See Jeremiah 31:34.) This is seen
again in Hebrews 8:11-12, "And they shall not teach one
another/ or say to each other, 'Know/ the Lord,'/ for they
shall all know me, / from the least of them to/ the greatest./
For I will be merciful towards their/iniquities,/and I will
remember their sins/no more."

In return, our responsibility is to remember God. (See
Deuteronomy 6:12, 8:18; Ecclesiastes 12:1; Psalm 103:2; and
Psalm 105:5.) Many of the psalms remind us to acknowledge
the generosity and goodness of the Lord. Psalm 78 (35) says
that the people remembered God was their rock, the Most
High God their redeemer.

God also is remembered through Jesus, the Second Person
of the Trinity. Saint Paul said to remember Jesus Christ, raised
from the dead (2 Timothy 2:8). Jesus himself told us that we
are to remember him. When he took the bread, gave thanks to
God, and broke it, he said, "This is my body, which is given for
you. Do this in remembrance of me" (Luke 22:19).

Remembering Jesus is vitally important for world peace. If
we remember Jesus at all times, committing sin is nearly
impossible. Jesus would be foremost in our thoughts, words,
and actions. We would see him in one another, and therefore,

treat each other with the utmost love and respect. Other
biblical instructions concern keeping the Sabbath day holy
(Exodus 20:8) and honoring our parents (Exodus 20:12). We
also are told to remember not to idol someone or something
other than God. (See Deuteronomy 4:23.)

So then, what we remember about our life is not so very
important, but rather, whom we remember is what counts. If
we want to remember the way that God remembers, we think
of one another as God thinks of us. This includes people who
do not remember us or need us. We remember our family and
friends as well as those most unlike us. We remember God in
the elderly, poor, homeless, hungry, naked, and sick through
works of mercy. We remember those in prison, out on the
battlefield, and in the ghettos. We also are to remember the
dead with a Christian burial and in our daily prayers requesting
that the Lord has mercy on their souls and that they rest in
eternal peace.

We do all of this in the present moment. We give glory and
honor to the Great I Am. And we enjoy the bounty of the
many blessings God gives us this very moment of this very day.

We are One Body

One of the greatest ways to strengthen our spirituality is by
passing it on. We cannot share what we do not know is within
us. In order to pass on our faith, we must recognize, name,
honor, and cherish it. The practice forces us to have a clear
understanding of our beliefs. We build on our own spirituality
when building it in others.

And in sharing our story of faith we share the story of God.
We evangelize and demonstrate the living God, our Heavenly
Father who works within the hearts and souls of all creation.
We move closer to being one with the Lord and one another.
We truly become one body in Christ.

Let us go to our elders and listen to their stories. Let us pass on their stories along with our own to younger generations. Tell friends and family how God worked in our lives. Then we must live the essence of that story of faith and be a living example of God's grace and glory, for this is the day the Lord has made. Let us rejoice and be glad.

Lord, I thank you for your presence in my life. May your Spirit guide me in spreading your holy name.

Our Spiritual Portfolio

What's in your spiritual portfolio?

We live in a materialistic world. Our worth as a person is equated with our income and possessions. If we lived a rich life, we have a lot of money, stocks, jewelry, a big house full of expensive furnishings, cars, and so on to show for our efforts. To the rest of the world we appear successful and wealthy. But this type of financial portfolio has a limited, one life-term return.

In contrast, our spiritual portfolio is an investment in eternity. Our ultimate worth is our connection to God. We are not only God's creation but God's beneficiary as well. We know that spirituality is one of the keys to a long, happy life. When we invest in our faith, we profit in this life and the next. The value of what we contribute towards our relationship with the Lord continues without end.

We do this by loving God with all of our heart, mind, and soul and loving and serving one another. Jesus said these were the most important things to do. Reach out to the poor and sick. Be a friend to the lonely and allow others to care for us. By sharing our love with those in need and accepting the care extended to us, we share in God's love.

The earthly world should draw progressively less of our attention as we age. We should continuously aim our focus on God. Some of this may occur naturally as we retire, move out of the big house, and lose the people we grew up with. Our attentions begin to move from this world and to the next.

Reflecting on his own life, Deacon Mike Zibrun from St. Peter Parish in Geneva, Illinois said that when he was younger, Christ was in whatever was left over from his busy day. His faith wasn't really in the moment. Now he strives always to be awesomely, beautifully, and overwhelming open to Christ. He finds this type of spirituality to be spontaneous, heartfelt, and humbling.

Every age is a blessing. God has a reason and a desire for each of us to live to a particular age. We should use our time wisely. Our senior years naturally offer many opportunities to do this. We may build on our relationship with the Lord through private and communal prayer; through the care we provide our loved ones; in our times of suffering and loss; and by sharing our story of faith.

We can call on the Holy Spirit to direct us. The New Testament clearly describes the Holy Spirit as the one who guides. Jesus carried out his ministry under the power of the Holy Spirit. Why not allow the Spirit to do the same for us? Why not ask the Holy Spirit, God's breath, to direct our sails until our last moment on earth and through eternity, into the arms of the Lord?

Lord, you are first, foremost, and always in my life. I center my thoughts on you.

Appendix

Suggestions for Compiling a Spiritual Autobiography

Your spiritual autobiography can be constructed in several ways. It may be more of a photo album; journal of personal writings; book of magazine and newspaper clippings; or a combination of some or all of these. Articles may be pasted or inserted in a spiral notebook or constructed into a scrapbook. Use your gifts and talents to tell your story of faith in ways most comfortable for you.

Consider including:
- The ways in which God answered your prayers
- The people who spiritually inspired you
- Your spiritual mentors and those you spiritually mentor
- What you learned from those you mentored
- People you were surprised to learn from
- Your many blessings
- The difficult times that later became your life-lessons
- The major turning points in your life
- Your reflections on the spiritual meaning of your life
- Ways in which your participation in church services promoted your spiritual growth
- The people in your faith community
- The ways in which you acted as a steward of the earth
- How you have promoted social justice
- The things you would do differently
- The sacred places where you feel spiritually moved
- Your favorite prayers and hymns
- Your favorite passages from Scripture and quotes from religious writings

- Your favorite saints from whom you petition prayers
- Your thoughts on death and the afterlife
- How you would like to be spiritually remembered

Patron Saints for Seniors

It times of trouble and illness, we pray to Jesus, the greatest healer and our merciful father. We also can call on Mary, Our Blessed Mother and greatest saint of all. We can ask our Guardian Angel or our patron saint to pray with us in all our needs as well.

Following are some of the conditions of aging experienced by many people as well as the saints that assist with prayers in these areas.

Abdominal Pain	Erasmus, Timothy
Aging	Apollonia
Alcoholics, Reformed	Martin of Tours, Matthias
Alcoholism	John of God, Martin of Tours, Matthias the Apostle, Monica
Ambulance Drivers	Michael the Archangel
Amputees	St. Anthony of Padua, Antony the Abbot
Anesthesiologists	Rene Goupil
Angina	Swithbert
Arm pain	Amalburga

Arthritis	Alphonsus, Maria de Liguori, James the Great
Bacterial Disease, Infections	Agrippina
Blindness	Cosmas, Damian, Lucy, Raphael the Archangel, Thomas the Apostle
Bowel Disorders	Bonaventure
Breast Cancer	Agatha, Aldegundis, Giles, Peregrine Laziosi, Mother Theodore Guerin/Theodora
Bruises, Bruising	Amalburga
Cancer	Peregrine Laziosi, Mother Theodore Guerin/Theodora
Caregivers	Elizabeth of Hungary, John of God, Martin de Porres, Rose of Lima, Aloysius Gonzaga
Causes, Lost, Impossible	Jude Thaddeus, Philomena, Rita of Cascia
Coughs	Blaise
Death	Michael the Archangel, Margaret, Joseph of Cuperntino
Dieticians	Martha
Disabilities	Giles, Seraphina

Disease, Contagious	Roch, Sebastian
Elderly People	Anthony of Padua
EMT, Paramedics	Michael the Archangel
Epilepsy	Valentine
Eyes, Eye Diseases	Aloysius Gonzaga, Clare of Assisi, Cyriacus, Herve, Lucy of Syracuse, Mother Theodore Guerin/Theodora, Odilia, Raphael the Archangel
Feet	Peter the Apostle, Servatus, Roch
Funeral Directors	Joseph of Arimathea, Sebastian
Gall Stones	Benedict
Gout	Andrew, Gregory the Great
Grandfathers	Joachim
Grandmothers	Anne
Head Injuries	John Licci
Headaches	Teresa of Avila
Healers	Brigid of Ireland, Raphael the Archangel
Health	Infant Jesus of Prague, Our Lady of Lourdes, Raphael the Archangel
Hearing	Francis de Sales, Cornelius

Heart Disease	John of God
Hemorrhages	Lucy of Syracuse
Herpes/Shingles	George, Anthony the Great
Hospital Workers	Basil the Great, Frances Xavier Cabrini, Elizabeth of Hungry, Camillus of Lellis, John of God, Jude
Hospitals	Camillus of Lellis, Elizabeth of Hungary, John of God, Jude Thaddeus, Vincent de Paul
Invalids	Roch
Kidney Disease	Benedict, Drogo, Margaret of Antioch, Ursus of Aosta, Ursus of Ravenna
Knee Troubles	Roch
Leg Disease	Servatus
Longevity	Peter the Apostle
Loneliness	Rita of Cascia
Loss of Parents	Dymphna, Elizabeth Ann Seton, Germaine Cousin, Margaret of Cortona, Maria Goretti, Teresa of Avila, Therese of Lisieux
Lungs, Respiratory	Bernadine of Siena, Theresa
Medical Technicians	Albert the Great

Mental Illness	Dymphna
Migraine	Gemma Galgani
Mothers	Mary, Anne, Monica
Neck, Stiff	Gemma Galgani
Neurological, Nerve Diseases	Bartholomew the Apostle, Dymphna
Nurses	Agatha, Camillus de Lellis, John of God
Pain	Gemma Galgani
Paralysis, Paralyzed	Alice, Osmund
Pharmacists	Cosmas, Damian, James the Greater, Raphael the Archangel
Physicians	Cosmas, Damian, Luke the Apostle, Pantaleon, Raphael the Archangel
Prolonged Suffering	Lydwina of Schiedam
Psychiatric Hospitals	Dymphna
Public Health	Martin de Porres
Radiologists	Michael the Archangel
Respiratory Problems	Bernadine of Siena
Skin Diseases	Antony the Abbott, Peregrine Laziosi, Roch

Stomach Diseases	Brice, Charles Borromeo, Timothy, Wolfgang
Strokes	Andrew Avellino, Wolfgang
Surgeons	Cosmas, Damian, Luke the Apostle, Roch
Throats	Andrew the Apostle, Blaise, Ignatius of Antioch, Lucy of Syracuse, Swithbert
Tuberculosis	Pantaleon, Therese of Lisieux
Widowers	Thomas More
Widows	Elizabeth of Hungary, Elizabeth of Portugal, Elizabeth Ann Seton, Margaret of Scotland, Paula, Rita of Cascia
Wounds	Aldegundis, Rita of Cascia

Prayers for Seniors

Memorare
Remember, O most gracious Virgin Mary, that never was it known that anyone who fled to your protection, implored your help, or sought your intercession was left unaided. Inspired by this confidence, I fly to you, O Virgin of virgins, my Mother! To you I come, before you I stand, sinful and sorrowful. O Mother of the Word Incarnate, despise not my petitions, but in your mercy, hear and answer me. Amen.

Morning Offering
O Jesus, through the Immaculate Heart of Mary, I offer you all of my prayers, works, and sufferings of this day in union with the Holy Sacrifice of the Mass throughout the world. I offer them for all the intentions of Your Sacred Heart: the salvation of souls, reparation for sin, the reunion of all Christians. I offer them for the intentions of our bishops and of all the Apostles of Prayer, and in particular for those recommended by our Holy Father this month. Amen.

The Simple Jesus Prayer
Lord Jesus Christ, Son of God, have mercy on me, a sinner.

Serenity Prayer
God grant me the serenity
to accept the things I cannot change;
courage to change the things I can;
and wisdom to know the difference.
Living one day at a time;
Enjoying one moment at a time;
Accepting hardships as the pathway to peace;
Taking, as He did, this sinful world
as it is, not as I would have it;
Trusting that He will make all things right
if I surrender to His Will;
That I may be reasonably happy in this life
and supremely happy with Him
forever in the next.
Amen.
-Reinhold Niebuhr

Prayer in Time of Sickness
Heavenly Father, I firmly believe you watch over us at all times
and that you would not allow senseless, needless suffering to
come to any of your dear children. I believe, therefore, that my
sickness is neither senseless nor needless. I trust you, knowing
that you would allow no cross to come my way without at the
same time offering me strength sufficient to carry it. Since
loving you is essentially a matter of accepting your will, I wish
to love you in my acceptance of this sickness. Indeed, I thank
you for this precious gift of sickness, because, in some way
known to you, it is for my good. Let me not squander this gift.
Finally, let me see it as sharing in the cross of Christ; let me so
accept and bear up under my poor health that it will be for the
good health of the body of Christ. If you should want me to go
on being an instrument in your hands for the good of others,
please restore me to good health. I ask in Christ's name, Amen.

Prayer for a Sick Family Member

Heavenly Father, we ask, if it be your will, that our sick one get well as soon as possible. In the meantime, may he/she understand that the pain and misery of sickness are good for us. May he come out of this sickness with a deeper compassion for all the suffering ones of the world, and be stronger to accept your will when even heavier crosses come his way. May he know the peace and joy of those who suffer willingly in union with the suffering Christ. We ask in His name. Amen.

Prayer for the Dying

Heavenly Father, look down with compassion on this suffering member of our family. May he/she be strengthened with your strength in the long hours that lie ahead. May he accept with serenity the anguish that you have allowed to come to him. May he be firmly convinced that his Brother, Christ, who knew far greater pain, will remain here by the bedside after we have gone. We ask, if it be your will, that our loved one be brought back to health. But if you wish to take him home to you, we will try to accept our loss in humble submission to your will. (Here let all present recite slowly and devoutly the Our Father, followed by the Hail Mary.)

Eternal Rest

Eternal rest grant to him, O Lord, and let perpetual light shine upon him; May his soul and the souls of all the faithful departed through the mercy of God rest in peace. Amen.

The Rosary
The rosary is a meditative and inspiring form of prayer.
Following is a list of all the prayers and mysteries of the rosary
in the order in which they are prayed. Choose one set of
mysteries: Joyful, Luminous, Sorrowful, or Glorious
throughout the rosary.

(For an easy way to pray, see *The Rosary Prayer by Prayer*. In
this book you simply can follow along prayer-by-prayer, page-
by-page.)

- Sign of the Cross

- Apostles Creed
- Our Father
- Three Hail Marys
- Glory Be

- First Mystery
  Joyful: Annunciation
  Luminous: Baptism of Jesus
  Sorrowful: Agony in the Garden
  Glorious: Resurrection
- Our Father
- 10 Hail Marys
- Glory Be

- Second Mystery
  Joyful: Visitation
  Luminous: Jesus' First Public Miracle
  Sorrowful: Scourging at the Pillar
  Glorious: Ascension
- Our Father
- 10 Hail Marys
- Glory Be

- Third Mystery
  Joyful: Nativity
  Luminous: Proclamation of the Kingdom of God
  Sorrowful: Crowning with Thorns
  Glorious: Descent of the Holy Spirit
- Our Father
- 10 Hail Marys
- Glory Be

- Fourth Mystery
  Joyful: Presentation
  Luminous: Transfiguration
  Sorrowful: Carrying of the Cross
  Glorious: Assumption of Mary
- Our Father
- 10 Hail Marys
- Glory Be

- Fifth Mystery
  Joyful: Finding in the Temple
  Luminous: Institution of the Eucharist
  Sorrowful: Crucifixion
  Glorious: Coronation of Mary
- Our Father
- 10 Hail Marys
- Glory Be

- Hail Holy Queen
- Sign of the Cross

Psalm 118

O give thanks to the LORD, for he is
    good;
  his steadfast love endures for ever!

Let Israel say,
  "His steadfast love endures for ever."
Let the house of Aaron say,
  "His steadfast love endures for ever."
Let those who fear the LORD say,
  "His steadfast love endures for ever."

Out of my distress I called on the LORD;
  The LORD answered me and set me
    in a broad place.
With the LORD on my side I do not fear.
  What can mortals do to me?
The LORD is on my side to help me;
  I shall look in triumph on those
    who hate me.
It is better to take refuge in the LORD
  than to put confidence in mortals.

It is better to take refuge in the LORD
  than to put confidence in princes.

All nations surrounded me;
  in the name of the LORD I cut them
    off!
They surrounded me, surrounded me
    on every side;
  In the name of the LORD I cut them
    off!
They surrounded me like bees;
  they blazed like a fire of thorns;

in the name of the LORD I cut them
    off!
I was pushed hard, so that I was
    falling,
  but the LORD helped me.
The LORD is my strength and my
    might;
  he has become my salvation.

There are glad songs of victory in the
    tents of the righteous;
"The right hand of the LORD does
    valiantly;
  the right hand of the LORD is
    exalted;
  the right hand of the LORD does
    valiantly;
I shall not die, but I shall live,
  and recount the deeds of the
    LORD.
The LORD has punished me severely,
  but he did not give me over to
    death.

Open to me the gates of
    righteousness,
  that I may enter through them
  and give thanks to the LORD.

This is the gate of the LORD;
  the righteous shall enter through it.

I thank you that you have answered
    me
  and have become my salvation.
The stone that the builders rejected

has become the chief cornerstone.
This is the LORD's doing;
    it is marvelous in our eyes.
This is the day that the LORD has
        made;
    let us rejoice and be glad in it.
Save us, we beseech you, O LORD!
    O LORD, we beseech you, give us
        success!

Blessed is the one who comes in the
        name of the LORD.
    We bless you from the house of the
        LORD.
The LORD is God,
    and he has given us light.
Bind the festal procession with
        branches,
    up to the horns of the altar.

You are my God, and I will give
        thanks to you;
    you are my God, I will extol you.

O give thanks to the LORD, for he is
        good,
    for his steadfast love endures for
        ever.

Resources

AARP
> http://www.aarp.org/
> 601 E Street N.W.
> Washington, DC 20049
>
> Toll-Free Nationwide:
> 1-888-OUR-AARP,
> 1-888-687-2277
> Toll-Free TTY: 1-877-434-7598

Alzheimer's Association
> www.alz.org
> Email: info@alz.org
> Helpline: 1-800-272-3900
>
> National Office
> 225 N. Michigan Ave., Fl 17
> Chicago, IL 60601-7633
>
> Advocacy/Public Policy
> 1212 New York Ave, NW
> Suite 800
> Washington, DC 20005-6105
> 1-202-393-7737
> advocate@alz.org

Administration on Aging (AOA) and Administration for
Community Living (ACL)
        http://www.aoa.gov/

        Mailing Address:
        Washington, DC 20201

        Physical Address:
        One Massachusetts Avenue, NW
        Washington, DC 20001

        1-202-401-4634

        Public Inquiries: 1-202-619-0724
        AOA Fax: 1-202-357-3555

        Eldercare Locator: 1-800-677-1116

        aclinfo@acl.hhs.gov

National Coalition on Aging
        Washington, D.C. 20036
        E-mail: info@ncoa.org
        1-800-424-9046

National Institute on Aging
        niaic@nia.nih.gov
        1-800-222-2225
        TTY: 1-800-222-4225

Social Security Administration
        http://www.ssa.gov/
        1-800-722-1213
        TTY 1-800-325-0778
        Office of Public Inquiries
        Windsor Park Building
        6401 Security Blvd
        Baltimore, MD 21235

Bibliography

Agnes, Michael. Editor in Chief. *Webster's New World College Dictionary*. New York: Macmillan, 1999.

Alzheimer's Association, 2008 Alzheimer's Disease Facts and Figures, Published in *Alzheimer's & Dementia*, Volume 4, Issue 2.

Arroyo, Raymond. *Mother Angelica. The Remarkable Story of a Nun, Her Nerve, and a Network of Miracles*. New York: Doubleday, 2005.

Atchley, Robert C. *Spirituality and Aging*. Baltimore: The John Hopkins University Press, 2009.

Bonhoeffer, Dietrich. *Ethics*. New York: Touchtone, 1955.

Catholic Online, www.catholic.org, Bakersfield, CA, 2009.

Cooke, Bernard. *Sacraments & Sacramentality*. Mystic, CT: Twenty-Third Publications, 2002.

Dossey, M.D., Larry. *Healing Words*. New York: Harper Collins, 1993.

Doyle, Mary K. *Grieving with Mary*. Skokie, IL: ACTA Publications, 2009.

Doyle, Mary K. *Mentoring Heroes*. Geneva, IL: 3E Press, 2000.

Doyle, Mary K. *The Rosary Prayer by Prayer*. Geneva, IL: 3E Press, 2006. (Now ACTA Publications.)

Doyle, Mary K. *Seven Principles of Sainthood*. Skokie, IL: ACTA Publications, 2008.

Ellsbert, Robert. *All Saints*. New York, IL: The Crossroad
Publishing Company, 1997.

Graham, Billy. *The Holy Spirit. Activating God's Power in Your Life*.
Thomas Nelson, 1988.

Hauerwas, Stanley, Carole Bailey Stoneking, Keith G. Meador
and David Cloutier (editors). *Growing Old in Christ*. Grand
Rapids, MI: Wm. B. Eerdmans Publishing C., 2003.

Hayflick, Ph.D., Leonard. *How and Why We Age*. New York:
Ballantine Books, 1994.

The Holy Bible. New Revised Standard Version Catholic Edition.
Oxford, New York: Oxford University Press, 1999.

Huels, J.C.D., John M. *The Pastoral Companion. A Canon Law
Handbook for Catholic Ministry*. Quincy, IL: Franciscan Press,
1995.

Hughes, Kathleen. *Saying Amen. A Mystagogy of Sacrament*.
Chicago: Archdiocese of Chicago, 1999.

Johnson, Elizabeth A. *Consider Jesus. Waves of Renewal in
Christology*. New York: The Crossroad Publishing Company,
1990.

Johnson, Elizabeth A. *The Church Women Want. Catholic Women
in Dialogue*. The Crossroad Publishing Company: New York,
2002.

Johnson, Elizabeth A. *She Who Is. The Mystery of God in Feminist
Theological Discourse*. The Crossroad Publishing Company: New
York, 2001.

Johnson, Ph.D., Richard P. *Creating a Successful Retirement.*
Liguori, Missouri; Liguori Lifespan, 1999.

Johnson, Richard P. *Parish Ministry for Maturing Adults.* New
London, CT: Twenty-Third Publications, 2007.

Kimble, Melvin (editor). *Aging, Spirituality, and Religion.* Volume
1. Minneapolis: Fortress Press, 1995.

Koenig Coste, Joanne. *Learning to Speak Alzheimer's. A
Groundbreaking Approach for Everyone Dealing with the Disease.* New
York: Houghton Miflin Company, 2003.

Kubler-Ross, Elisabeth and David Kessler. *Life Lessons. Two
Experts on Death and Dying Teach Us About the Mysteries of Life and
Living.* New York: Scribner, 2000.

Libreria Editrice Vaticana. *Catechism of the Catholic Church.*
Dubuque, IA: Brown-Roa, 1994.

Macarthur, John. *Twelve Extraordinary Women. How God Shaped
Women of the Bible and What He Wants to Do with You.* Nashville:
Thomas Nelson, 2005.

Mace, M.A., Nancy L. and Peter V. Rabins, M.D., M.P.H. *The
36-Hour Day.* New York: John Hopkins University Press and
Wellness Central, 1999.

McGrath, Alister E. *Christian Spirituality.* Malden, MA:
Blackwell Publishers, Inc., 1999.

Moberg, Ph.D., David O. *Aging and Spirituality. Spiritual
Dimensions of Aging Theory, Research, Practice, and Policy.* New
York: The Haworth Pastoral Press, 2001.

Northrup, M.D., Christiane. *The Wisdom of Menopause. Creating Physical and Emotional Health and Healing During the Change.* New York: Bantam Books, 2001.

Northrup, M.D., Christiane. *Women's Bodies, Women's Wisdom. Creating Physical and Emotional Health and Healing.* New York: Bantam Books, 1998.

Ray, Oakley. Vanderbilt University. "How the Mind Hurts and Heals the Body." *American Psychologist,* January 2004.

Roizen, M.D., Michael F. and Mehmet C. Oz, M.D. *You Staying Young. The Owner's Manual for Extending Your Warranty.* New York: Free Press, 2007.

Rowe, M.D., John W. and Robert L. Kahn, Ph.D. *Successful Aging.* New York: Dell Publishing, 1998.

Schreck, Alan. *Your Life in the Holy Spirit. What every Catholic Needs to Know and Experience.* Ijamsville, Maryland: The Word Among Us, 1995.

Snowdon, Ph.D., David. *Aging with Grace. What the Nun Study Teaches Us About Living Longer, Healthier, and More Meaningful Lives.* New York: Bantam Books, 2001.

St Anthony Messenger online, http://americancatholic.org

Stanley, Charles F. *Living in the Power of the Holy Spirit.* Nashville: Nelson Books, 2005.

Stravinskas, Ph.D., S.T.D., Reverend Peter M.J. *Catholic Dictionary.* Huntington, IN: Our Sunday Visitor Publishing Division, Our Sunday Visitor, Inc., 2002.

"Taking Care of the Caregiver." www.mayoclinic.com: Mayo Foundation for Medical Education and Research, February 3, 2009.

Wicks, Robert J. and Richard D. Parsons, Donald Capps, Editors. *Clinical Handbook of Pastoral Counseling Volume 1*. Mahwah, New Jersey: Paulist Press, 1993.

Wicks, Robert J. Editor. *Handbook of Spirituality for Ministers*. New York: Paulist Press, 1995.

Acknowledgements

With deepest gratitude, I wish to acknowledge those who helped me bring this book to fruition especially my daughter, Erin Lukasiewicz, and sister, Patricia Brewer, who read all of my manuscripts several times before anyone else. They are an essential part in building my books.

In addition, thank you to my cousin, Debra McElroy, who read through one of the versions of this book and offered her expert medical advice as well as my brother, John Doyle, for numerous resources and sharing his experience of working with the aging population.

Thank you also to my fabulous editor, Charles Fiore, for making me a better writer, and cover designer, Chuck Romano, for *Young in the Spirit's* striking cover.

I also am grateful to Deacon Michael Zebrun, Mary Roger Madden, S.P., and all those who answered my questionnaire as well as my friend and mentor, Alexa Suelzer, S.P. They added greatly to my understanding and information.

In addition, thank you to Michele Sylvestro and Lynn Klika at Catholic Word, Jean Zander at St. Catherine of Sienna Press, and Greg Pierce at ACTA publications for their guidance on publication as well as Greg's help with distribution.

Most of all I am thankful to the Lord for blessing me with my loving husband, Marshall, and our large family and circle of friends. My dear children, Lisa, Erin, and Joseph; children-in-law, Mark, Steve, and Aurelie; grandsons, Daniel and Tyler; and my sisters, brothers, brothers-in-law, sisters-in-law; step-children, and step-grandchildren are constant sources of love and support. They fill my heart.